THE LONG PALE CORRIDOR

CONTEMPORARY POEMS OF BEREAVEMENT

EDITED BY JUDI BENSON & AGNETA FALK

BLOODAXE BOOKS

ISBN: 1 85224 317 1

First published 1996 by
Bloodaxe Books Ltd,
P.O. Box 1SN,
Newcastle upon Tyne NE99 1SN.

Bloodaxe Books Ltd acknowledges
the financial assistance of Northern Arts.

Cover printing by J. Thomson Colour Printers Ltd, Glasgow.

Printed in Great Britain by
Bell & Bain Limited, Glasgow, Scotland.

THE LONG PALE CORRIDOR

CONTENTS

V Holes, spaces...

VII Someone is dressing up for death today, a change of skirt or tie...

FOREWORD

For much of this century death and grief have been taboo subjects: not to be spoken of, or referred to only with hushed or oblique references. Doctors, nurses and others involved in health care have been party to this taboo. My training at medical school led me to see death always as a failure. The modern hospice and palliative care movement, which owes much to the pioneering vision of Dame Cicely Saunders, has since its origins sought to change this taboo. The movement strove to affirm life while regarding dying as a normal process, as well as to relieve pain and symptoms, to integrate the psychological, social and spiritual aspects of a person's care and to support patients to live as actively as possible until death. Perhaps even more significantly, attention turned to the needs of the close family and friends – to help them during the patient's illness and during their own grief. This was a turning point for medicine, which had hitherto been concerned exclusively with the patient.

What can poetry offer in all this? Poetry's subject is life and all that happens in it, poetry opens a window into our emotions and struggles. So in this excellent collection, where modern poets grapple with personal grief, they can deepen our understanding and help us whether we are doctors, nurses, social workers, ministers, friends trying to be with someone who grieves, or when we ourselves grieve.

In my work at University College Hospital, London, at St Joseph's Hospice, Hackney and as a doctor within a community palliative care team, I was often surprised by what gave comfort. Just as every person is different, so every relationship is different and every grief is different. A nurse colleague from a hospice in Belfast told me that often relatives chose to have the opening poem in this collection – Dylan Thomas's 'Do Not Go Gentle into That Good Night' – read at the funeral. The poem is a tirade against death. But so many fight death. The poem is as relevant today as when it was written. Mimi Khalvati echoes the form in her un-rhymed villanelle.

One of the greatest strengths of this collection is the vast range of deep emotions found within; the pain of loss or seeing someone suffer, anger, rage at the world or at the person who died for leaving us, disbelief, shock, the bewilderment of losing a friend or parent, denial – this hasn't happened – guilt – at something that wasn't said – fear, isolation, disorganisation – when the whole world seems unimportant – acceptance and humour.

Several poets question our assumptions of how we want those we love to behave. Some deal with stillbirth, the death of a child, death from AIDS, death from suicide. Some deal with topics which are uncomfortable for us to witness, to watch or to experience – the poet is searching their own emotions for truth. So while many of the poems will provide comfort and may help to understand how we react, many will challenge those of us doctors, nurses, social workers or friends about how and what we do.

Several poems deal with the shock and bewilderment of losing a friend or parent in a concentration camp or in war. Patricia Bishop writes about the difficulty of breaking the news of a child's death to the parents. You will find doctor poets, such as Dannie Abse, writing about the deaths of those they love. A short poem by Pamela Gillilan shows how the little things that are said can be so important.

There is humour too. For example, Bruce Dawe recounts how his mother-in-law would react to her funeral. In his attempts to register a death, Douglas Dunn, found himself in the wrong room with a wedding party!

The anthology moves through several stages in grieving. After the shock and rage against dying, and the pain of seeing a loved one suffer, as in Ken Smith's poem 'Milly's End', comes the pain of returning to mundane living – including the silence as in John Figueroa's poem. W.H. Auden describes how, in grief, nothing in the universe seems as important – 'The stars are not wanted now: put out every one'. Poets recount the feeling of loss. For instance, Anne Sexton, writing in a poem dedicated to her mother and father who died within three months of each other.

But there is one emotion that is in every poem – that of love. As a young doctor, I remember reading, in a book by Dr James Hanratty (former medical director of St Joseph's Hospice) that 'grief is the price paid for love'. He went on to explain how platitudes such as 'time will cure', 'go away for a holiday to help you to forget', 'don't keep dwelling on it', are meaningless and can be hurtful. In today's fast moving society the grieving person may be supported by friends and family for the first month or two, but then often is expected to get on with life. In hospitals or in general practice, where we may feel under pressure to treat more people and be more efficient, we may feel we have too little time to spend listening and talking with patients and their families. In this anthology the poets remind us that the scar of grief can always remain, when they write about it after two years, four years, six years, twenty years. Some may even – as Oktay Rifat does in his poem – attempt to give the person a life within their hands and eyes.

There is much that the person who has died can leave behind. In the last section of this anthology 'Someone is dressing up for death today, a change of skirt or tie' poets write in the voice of the one who is dying or about their own death. Thus, Judi Benson's and Agneta Falk's selection as a whole ends on an optimistic note. For even if we have no beliefs in an afterlife, those whom we grieve have left a rich legacy – not least in the love we keep alive for them. It is important that in this arresting volume, this love is expressed by poets, for poetry is not only the recollection of emotion but its communication to other people.

DR IRENE HIGGINSON
Senior Lecturer/Consultant

INTRODUCTION

'What struck me was the realisation that this "enormous" thing happening in your life, losing someone you love, is such a "normal" occurrence, and yet we don't know how to deal with it.' – AGNETA FALK

Death is a common shared experience, unavoidable and inevitable for us all; yet it remains one of the most difficult topics to talk about. As a bereavement counsellor with the Royal London Hospital's Bereavement Service, it became clear to me that every bereavement is different, just as every relationship is different. The circumstances of a death can have a great effect on the adjustment to loss, just as one's own philosophy and inner resources, and the amount of support available, can be a hindrance or a help. At the same time, there were many similarities. Whether an individual had support or not, the overriding 'feeling' was that there was 'no one to talk to'; 'no one understands'. Some people felt that they 'had to be strong'. As a result, very often grief was delayed or denied, only to surface years later causing great confusion and self-doubt. 'Why do I feel like this, it's been five years. I must be crazy'. There can be tremendous despair with the loss of a loved one, when life no longer feels worth living, and indeed thoughts of 'ending it all' may be entertained, coupled with intense shame for having such thoughts.

While death can happen in an instant, grief takes time and there is no limit to the time it takes. Grief is not linear with stages and phases to be got through and left behind. Rather, it is a circular whirlpool of emotion and often these emotions are contradictory. Feelings ebb and flow and flood in again when least expected, knocking the bereaved sideways once again. Dr Colin Murray Parkes describes grief as 'the greatest mental anguish...for which there is no anaesthetic'. We cannot give the bereaved what they most want; to have their loved one back. Yet it can help to know that others have suffered such pain and survived. It was this notion of shared experience that led us to consider putting together a collection of bereavement poems.

Poets have always written about death, about grief, daring to give expression to the unthinkable, in an effort to make sense of it all. And more than any other genre, poetry is the one the bereaved turn to for comfort; for this ability to express the deepest most painful feelings. Attitudes to death have changed over the years as have our rituals and ceremonies, the time allowed for grieving. Agneta Falk and I wanted poems which would reflect the world we live in; knowing that many fine older poems had already been collected in anthologies and therefore were available to be treasured and rediscovered. We narrowed our focus to contemporary poems on bereavement; even so, there were many poems we could not include. Initially, it felt a daunting venture to put together such a collection and yet we knew this was precisely the sort of book the bereaved would turn to.

We particularly wanted poems written from personal experience as opposed to general statements about death. Of the many books I came across as a counsellor, it was the ones reflecting personal experience that most struck me and to which I returned again and again (e.g. C.S. Lewis' *A Grief Observed*; Lily Pincus' *Death in the Family*; Rebecca Abrams' *When Parents Die*).

In this collection, poets express a range of emotions: rage, shock, fear, disbelief, despair, guilt, blame, remorse, relief, loneliness, numbness and sometimes humour. They share their philosophies, their memories, what it felt like for them a year after the death... or two years, five years, twenty years later.

There are poems dealing with the illness that leads to death; long years of caring for the dying. Poems that give attention to the 'arrangements', the funeral, the cremation and a few that reflect the added pain of not having a body to bury, and thus not being able to say goodbye; holding out the hope that perhaps there has been some mistake and this is all a bad dream from which they will awake.

I depended greatly on Agneta's own experiences of bereavement to give insight and clear judgement, just as I relied on her expertise as a poet. While we were coming at this from quite different perspectives, there was a lot of common ground. There were times of great sadness in reading these poems, when our own sorrows were recalled. At the same time, we encountered such love and affection in these poems that we came to look upon this book as a celebration of life, however brief. I know there were times when we felt quite alone in what we were attempting. Being able to share such doubts was invaluable.

While we tried to include as wide a range of experiences as possible, we know that not everyone's situation will be represented. Our hope is that in some way these poems will reach out across the abyss and give voice to the unspeakable in an effort to show that however isolated one feels, that we are not in fact entirely alone. There is tremendous courage and faith in these poems as poets confront their own mortality and all that they will leave behind. And through it all has come a heightened appreciation of life and all those we love.

JUDI BENSON

INTRODUCTION

It wasn't until I experienced bereavement myself that I realised what a different world you enter. It's the day you lose your innocence. Never again can you take anything for granted. The questions of life and death are now for real. Life takes on a new significance. You are looking for comfort, anything to make sense of losing someone you love.

There can be great dignity in death. Many people who have shared those last moments with a dying person have felt strengthened by it. I did.

What struck me was the realisation that this "enormous" thing happening in your life, losing someone you love, is such a "normal" occurrence that we don't know how to deal with it. There are no guidelines. Needing to talk about the experience takes you over the same ground again and again. You are left with a lot of questions to which there are few answers, except time.

There is so much to come to terms with and it's a lonely painful path. There is only so much other people can take – you put on a mask in the outside world, so as not to burden them. Later you suffer the consequences for having bottled it all up and the emotions spill out in private. You become aware of how difficult it is for some people to approach you, as they are afraid they might use the wrong words, afraid of disturbing you, and in the process you feel even more isolated. Although I have suffered bereavement myself, I still find it difficult to face someone else's grief.

But a death isn't only about sadness; it is also a celebration of someone's life, a heightened awareness of that particular person's uniqueness. It's perhaps the first time we fully realise what the person who died meant to us, making us aware of what a life is worth.

When Judi Benson and I first talked about putting this anthology together, we were not always sure it was the right thing to do. We thought perhaps the concentration of so many poems on bereavement might be overwhelming, but as we progressed through the anthology we became more certain of the value of this book. I remembered how I had myself read *A Grief Observed* by C.S. Lewis again and again, leaning on every word and feeling less alone for being able to identify with his experience.

Some of the poems we received were naturally very personal, very raw. We almost felt they needed to rest for a while before being shared so publicly. At the same this is precisely why they are so good, so immediate; precisely why they will be of comfort to people who have experienced bereavement and also touch people who have not yet experienced it.

The process of finding poems has not been hard. The difficulty has been to know where to draw the line, not wanting to exclude poems we felt belonged in this anthology. No doubt we will have missed some we would have wanted to include, but those poems still exist elsewhere in their own right.

Judi's experience as a bereavement counsellor was of great help in times of doubt. With such range and intensity of emotion, as expressed in many of these poems, one can easily lose sight of the whole: the whole being a richly textured tribute to life.

The Long Pale Corridor is about love, anger, pain, underpinned with humour. The wealth of life and the clarity with which it is expressed cannot fail to move one profoundly. It also fills one with tremendous hope, because however bad grief may be, it is never meaningless.

AGNETA FALK

GRIEF

It's always by the sea
the waves, the storm.
Bidding the salty water
to flood the long pale
corridor on nothingness.

Agneta Falk

I. Do not go gentle into that good night...

DYLAN THOMAS
Do Not Go Gentle into That Good Night

Do not go gentle into that good night,
Old age should burn and rave at close of day;
Rage, rage against the dying of the light.

Though wise men at their end know dark is right.
Because their words have forked no lightning they
Do not go gentle into that good night.

Good men, the last wave by, crying how bright
Their frail deeds might have danced in a green bay,
Rage, rage against the dying of the light.

Wild men who caught and sang the sun in flight,
And learn, too late, they grieved it on its way,
Do not go gentle into that good night.

Grave men, near death, who see with blinding sight
Blind eyes could blaze like meteors and be gay,
Rage, rage against the dying of the light.

And you, my father, there on the sad height,
Curse, bless, me now with your fierce tears, I pray.
Do not go gentle into that good night.
Rage, rage against the dying of the light.

ASA BENVENISTE
Falling

Window open on the shadows
that shape the sun's distance,
closer today than it's ever been
this year. That's what shimmer
does, and the vulnerable drag on my leg.
Blood falling like pollenous sap through
the bandages. I am now in
the throes of a new language you (she)
will never learn from its banal
precocity. I'm sorry for this stupid
trip, pulling the trigger myself
for the second time as I reached
for the open window, looking down
at my only foot.
                    'Un homme
qui veut se mutiler.'
                         Like coming
to the cut of the pad; in any case
there are no other poems, the wind too
has fallen, the line of birds
above the colour of trees
and of deepening blood which persuades me
into believing that I am still one piece.

Weather Change

This time of year,
day pursuing the window
wiper, cobwebs, seeds already
on all the paper poems
becoming contiguous
(I'm trying to describe dust).

And death too
just down the slope,
smell of bacon
frying in a dirty pipe
and wet leather.
In the pane
there goes the fat man,
peg trousers,
painted lips.
Time to look into fear
again. The coordinates:
twenty intersecting
lines on the track
of marvellous errors.

Trajectory

Where do these golden clips
come from? Six shells. No gun.
Their inadequacies express
nothing but politics,
a broken plank across
the canal at the bottom
of indefinition.

        When I wake
I find all the words crossed out.
Life with a three-legged dog.
So much for identities,
falling, drowned,
disappearing against the colours
of the campaign poster.

There's no way to start again,
too many dead lighters around,
too many blanks.
Aren't there shapelier bullets than this?

ANNA FISSLER
responses

1

here we are
at the edge
of each other
needing
some kind of touching
of the heart
more than the flesh

we curve around
this space between us

this space between us
the deepest understanding

2

here
I am here
in this white room
surrounded
by a clock
smashing out time

I am here waiting
hoping
for one man
to open the door
and bring me a miracle

3

I am here
full-grown, full-lipped, alive, pulsating.
My breath, hot, violent, catches in my throat.
I see my face in the surgeon's eyes.
It does not betray me.
I am grateful that he does not look away.
I need to fix my gaze on him, his eyes.
I want to laugh, moan, turn away,
but his eyes transfix me

reinforce his words,
show me there is no mistake.
She squeezes my hand, the nurse,
holds it cupped in her own hands.
It is cold,
limp, strangely innocent in her healthy fingers.
I am dulled suddenly, changed.
The world is all at once tighter.

(untitled)

we will never
have any memory
of dying
yet I know its scent
can taste its sweat
feel its cool breath
on my shoulder
meet its dark eyes –
no stranger to me

we will never
have any memory
of dying
no matter
living is the sum
total

we busy ourselves
with things
we can never know
miss what is here
within our grasp
search with gloved hands
for the intangible

you are here
I am here

it is enough.

MICHAEL BLACKBURN
from The Stone Ship

7

This is our stone ship
sailing where the earth goes.
The sound of my father's cough
leaks into my room.
His heart is a sad engine,
you can hear it hiss and click.
The black map of the constellations
slides across my window,
calm and cruel and out of reach
as I lie awake in my tight room
in our stone ship
sailing where the earth goes.
Three foot thick our old walls
ooze damp, florescing darkly
miles from any sea.
The sound of my father's cough
leaks into my room.
His heart is a sad engine
fumbling its beat.
This is our stone ship
sailing where the earth goes
through coughs and constellations.
Our leaky ship.
Our sad engines.

11

Whisky and cigarettes
and love were your comforts, though love
moved invisible as air about you
and whisky did for you
and cigarettes did for you
and the body's inborn faults did for you
and surgery and drugs
could not sustain you
as much as love, the transparent one,
the virtue evading words
like light, the uncatchable traveller,

that makes all things visible
and warms where it falls like a mother's hand.

But even light grows old and small
outliving the stars it flies from.

And bodies fall to ash.

PHILIP HODGINS
Death Who

The conversation with cancer
begins equitably enough.
You and he are summing each other up,
trading ripostes and *bon mots*
before the soup.
Everything seems ordinary.
There is interest and boredom,
and you've been drinking all afternoon
which could mean that you're depressed
or that you're in good form.
You get each other's measure
and the conversation settles,
subjects divide and increase like cells.
Gradually you realise
that like the background Mozart
all the emotions are involved,
and that you're no longer saying as much.
Put it down to strength of intent.
He's getting aggressive
and you're getting tired. Someone
says he's a conversational bully
but you're fascinated.
He tells you things about yourself,
forgotten things and those not yet found out,
pieces from childhood and the unhealing wound.
It's all there.

Forgetting food, you drink (too much
red wine will encourage nightmares
but that's not a problem now), you marvel.
Isn't he tireless!
A raconteur like something out of Proust.
He blows cigar smoke into your face
and makes a little joke.
It's actually too much.
You're tired and the more you tire
the more the words are everywhere.
You go and recline on the couch,
but he won't shut up. He follows you there
and makes the cushions uncomfortable for you.
It's so unjust.
Your host is in the kitchen,
all the guests have gone
and the cancer's got you like conviction
and he's kneeling on your chest,
glaring over you,
pushing a cushion into your face,
talking quietly and automatically,
the words not clear.
He's got you and he's really pushing,
pushing you to death.

BEN OKRI
To One Dying of Leukaemia
(for F.H.)

Your dream of another
Life is before you.
They have drawn the curtain
Tighter from within.
The flowers in your veins
Grow rot while
They flow with their petals
Of life
Upon your waning face.

Your dream of another
Life is before you.

Mother surrounds you
With panic.
Her desire is to share
Your deflowering Rot
Of fate.
They now play charades before you:
Of all the happy days
In memory
The wondrous journeys
To the exotic place where
The sickle falls.
They act out fantasies
For you
They bring on childhood
Friends
And surround you with
The memories
Of Old China.

And yet you know
That your dream of another
Life is before you.
They do not know
Your terror.
Their twists of love
Are like tender innocence
With fangs that
Fear death
And fear you.
They no longer share
Your hunger
For rich tapestries
And fashion fingers
Weighted with rings
Of pearl and jade
Or for the smell
Of jasmine tea
On a wintry day.

They process you
In stories
To friends.
They no longer share
The fastening
Of your eyes.
They do not see things
As you do
With the special
Sadness
Of one at the blue
Door
Departing without
A smile.
They fear your
Grey eyes
That gaze now

JUDI THWAITE
For Mark

I cradle you back into me
try to feed you with my body
my firstborn that now finds
it so hard to play
you are leaking away from me
I can't stop it
                someone help me

You bear it with the mantle of old age
the sickness   the burning ulcers
I see in your weary face
the muteness of starving children
your quiet acceptance
as you try to make sense of
your frightening world

ajumbleofneedlesandpain
I am helpless
my body hurts
as I stroke your wilting skin
and watch you with a smile
that fronts my tears
at night – away from me –
your cry echoes in my head

      'Mummy make me well'

DOUGLAS DUNN
Thirteen Steps and the Thirteenth of March

She sat up on her pillows, receiving guests.
I brought them tea or sherry like a butler,
Up and down the thirteen steps from my pantry.
I was running out of vases.

More than one visitor came down, and said,
'Her room's so cheerful. She isn't afraid.'
Even the cyclamen and lilies were listening,
Their trusty tributes holding off the real.

Doorbells, shopping, laundry, post and callers,
And twenty-six steps up the stairs
From door to bed, two times thirteen's
Unlucky numeral in my high house.

And visitors, three, four, five times a day;
My wept exhaustions over plates and cups
Drained my self-pity in these days of grief
Before the grief. Flowers, and no vases left.

Tea, sherry, biscuits, cake, and whisky for the weak...
She fought death with an understated mischief –
'I suppose I'll have to make an effort' –
Turning down painkillers for lucidity.

Some sat downstairs with a hankie
Nursing a little cry before going up to her.
They came back with their fears of dying amended.
'Her room's so cheerful. She isn't afraid.'

Each day was duty round the clock.
Our kissing conversations kept me going,
Those times together with the phone switched off,
Remembering our lives by candlelight.

John and Stuart brought their pictures round,
A travelling exhibition. Dying,
She thumbed down some, nodded at others,
An artist and curator to the last,

Honesty at all costs. She drew up lists,
Bequests, gave things away. It tore my heart out.
Her friends assisted at this tidying
In a conspiracy of women.

At night, I lay beside her in the unique hours.
There were mysteries in candle-shadows,
Birds, aeroplanes, the rabbits of our fingers,
The lovely, erotic flame of the candlelight.

Sad? Yes. But it was beautiful also.
There was a stillness in the world. Time was out
Walking his dog by the low walls and privet.
There was anonymity in words and music.

She wanted me to wear her wedding ring.
It wouldn't fit even my little finger.
It jammed on the knuckle. I knew why
Her fingers dwindled and her rings slipped off.

After the funeral, I had them to tea and sherry
At the Newland Park. They said it was thoughtful.
I thought it was ironic – one last time –
A mad reprisal for their loyalty.

LOTTE KRAMER
Visit

In May she knew
These were the steep
Hours of her dying.

By her bedside
We talked of apples
We would pick
In her orchard
In the autumn,

Legitimate lies
Fighting cold vertigo;
We need that solace
To see us through
Her intelligent presence.

Hospital Visit

Grief in this dustless ward
Dwarfing all fears
Of present wounds. Her eyes
Know boundless night,
No fleshly loss of limb.
'It grows with age.'
Such proof again of time's
Dull healing lie.
'My children died at Auschwitz.'
Nothing else.
Here sunlight and the groans
Of surgery,
And my fermenting tears
Have bones of shame.

PETER ABBS

A Conversation with the Doctor at the Time of the Chernobyl Disaster

You stand at the window in your striped pyjamas,
Like a disaster victim, and I am outside.
It is the second of May. The hawthorn blossom
Froths and blows all over Sheringham.
The doctor takes me to his car and says:
Your father hasn't much longer to go.
Over our heads the arctic clouds explode.
And mushroom. *He has the worst heart I know.*
The wind, unseen, plucks at our hair and clothes.
He is living on borrowed time. And pills.
I catch you at the window waiting for news.
There is nothing, nothing more medicine can do.

You turn to me, taciturn: *What did he say?*
And all about us spreads cancerous May.

November Garden

This November's slow. An ageing sun weeps cold
On stone. You remain an invalid in bed.
Your body's shrunk. You lie small as a child.
I won't fucking mend this time, you said.
Your mind meanders through a maze its own.
The clinical air blasts my face and head.
And all you want is to be left alone.

This garden's become a place I almost dread.
A rectangle of smoking foliage. More gaps
Than substance. What fruit remains is cut and hollow.
The weight of barren years drags down my steps.
I recall early frosts, the drifting snow,
Snow that, once, as we walked, filled in our tracks –
Snow that was always driving in, behind our backs.

JAMES DICKEY
The Hospital Window

I have just come down from my father.
Higher and higher he lies
Above me in a blue light
Shed by a tinted window.
l drop through six white floors
And then step out onto pavement.

Still feeling my father ascend,
I start to cross the firm street,
My shoulder blades whining with all
The glass the huge building can raise.
Now I must turn round and face it.
And know his one pane from the others.

Each window possesses the sun
As though it burned there on a wick.
I wave, like a man catching fire.
All the deep-dyed windowpanes flash,
And, behind them, all the white rooms
They turn to the color of Heaven.

Ceremoniously, gravely, and weakly,
Dozens of pale hands are waving
Back, from inside their flames.
Yet one pure pane among these
Is the bright, erased blankness of nothing.
I know that my father is there.

In the shape of his death still living.
The traffic increases around me
Like a madness called down on my head.
The horns blast at me like shotguns,
And drivers lean out, driven crazy –
But now my propped-up father

Lifts his arm out of stillness at last.
The light from the window strikes me
And I turn as blue as a soul,
As the moment when I was born.
I am not afraid for my father –
Look! He is grinning; he is not

Afraid for my life, either,
As the wild engines stand at my knees
Shredding their gears and roaring,
And I hold each car in its place
For miles, inciting its horn
To blow down the walls of the world

That the dying may float without fear
In the bold blue gaze of my father.
Slowly I move to the sidewalk
With my pin-tingling hand half dead
At the end of my bloodless arm.
I carry it off in amazement,

High, still higher, still waving,
My recognised face fully mortal,
Yet not; not at all, in the pale,
Drained, otherworldly, stricken,
Created hue of stained glass.
I have just come down from my father.

MIMI KHALVATI
Coma

Mr Khalvati? Larger than life he was;
too large to die so they wired him up on a bed.
Small as a soul he is on the mountain ledge.

Lids gone thin as a babe's. If it's mist he sees
it's no mist he knows by name. *Can you hear me,
Mr Khalvati?* Larger than life he was

and the death he dies large as the hands that once
drowned mine and the salt of his laugh in the wave.
Small as a soul he is on the mountain ledge.

Can you squeeze my hand? (Ach! Where are the hands
I held in mine to pull me back to the baize?)
Mr Khalvati? Larger than life he was

with these outstretched hands that squeezing squeeze
thin air. Wired he is, tired he is and there,
small as a soul he is on the mountain ledge.

No nudging him out of the nest. No one to help him
fall or fly, there's no coming back to the baize.
Mr Khalvati? Larger than life he was.
Small as a soul he is on the mountain ledge.

HEATHER HAND
Thirteen Days to Christmas

So you got on with the business
of living, stripping the house down
painting it back up again. Even
putting on weight. That was not
the treatment. *Was it was it?*

Then the breathing grew thick, clumsy,
the lumps increased. *What do you think?*
your voice, that day in the kitchen
the blue sweat-shirt rolled round
your neck. Your right hand pointing at heaven

your left hand stroking the armpit
the smooth glossy surface of that lump.
I could not help but touch. Comfort.

Thirteen days to Christmas
and I'm following the trolley
through the doors of the hospice.

A wave of oxygen feeding you
till the lungs fill up and the tube
fixed to the machine is sipping
those bluish mouthfuls of fluid
into the glass, filling and emptying.

Leaning over the bed, your sister,
holding your hand as she hasn't
done since you were 2, 3, 5.
She peels back the sheet, to see
that your colour is right, cupping
those cooled feet in her hands
rubbing rubbing. Then she runs
a paper towel under the tap
under your arms, neck, lips,
every silver crease of the body.

And I think of how the cow
peels away the delicate lining
of the birth sac, licking
those layers of grease away
from the body; making sure
that it is seen to, properly,
that you were loved.

THOM GUNN
Memory Unsettled

Your pain still hangs in air,
Sharp motes of it suspended;
The voice of your despair –
That also is not ended:

When near your death a friend
Asked you what he could do,
'Remember me,' you said.
We will remember you.

Once when you went to see
Another with a fever
In a like hospital bed,
With terrible hothouse cough
And terrible hothouse shiver
That soaked him and then dried him,
And you perceived that he
Had to be comforted,

You climbed in there beside him
And hugged him plain in view,
Though you were sick enough,
And had your own fears too.

ROY FISHER
As He Came Near Death

As he came near death things grew shallower for us:
We'd lost sleep and now sat muffled in the scent of tulips, the
      medical odours, and the street sounds going past,
      going away;
And he, too, slept little, the morphine and the pink light the
      curtains let through floating him with us,
So that he lay and was worked out on to the skin of his life and
      left there,
And we had to reach only a little way into the warm bed to scoop
      him up.

A few days, slow tumbling escalators of visitors and cheques, and
      something like popularity;
During this time somebody washed him in a soap called *Narcissus*
      and mounted him, frilled with satin, in a polished case.

Then the hole: this was a slot punched in a square of plastic grass
      rug, a slot lined with white polythene, floored with dyed
      green gravel.

The box lay in it we rode in the black cars round a corner, got out
into our coloured cars and dispersed in easy stages.

After a time the grave got up and went away.

PAUL DURCAN
Cot

We cringed around your bed in the hospital ward.
The matron announced you would die in half an hour.
She spoke as if dictating from a train timetable.
Always in Italy the trains run on time.
I was dispatched to telephone the relations
But visitors to the dying had access only to a payphone.
None of the family had any change.
I had to borrow two tenpenny pieces
From the matron who had scheduled your death.
The first payphone did not work but the second did.
The relations said they would be with us in no time.
When I came scuttling back into the ward
And peered over the shoulders of my brothers and sisters
I saw that the deathbed had become a cot
And that you, Daddy, were a small, agèd infant
Strugglng to stay alive in the world.
You were kicking up your legs in the air,
Brandishing your bony white knuckles.
I realised that you were my newborn son.
What kind of a son will you be to me?
Will you be as faithful a son to me
As you have been a father?
As intimate, as funny, as alien?
As furry, as skinny, as flighty?

Old man, infant boy,
As you writhe there
On your backside
In your cot
How helpless you are,

A minuscule helplessness
Heaving with innocence;
A baby dinosaur
With an expiry date.
You begin to bawl.
My mother takes off her black glove
And lays her hand
Across your threadbare skull.
You wave her goodbye,
She who loves you
After one day
And forty-four years.
You go back to sleep,
The black world to rue.
Bonny boys are few.
Don't fret son,
Don't ever again fret yourself.

HEATHER HAND
Hospice

You did not shine. You did not
walk through the pearly white gate
and ask for admittance.
You lie on your side,
your body still working
as if you had climbed out
of the body, exhausted.

The white sheet laid
under the head to catch
the saliva. That did not shine.
So we talked, softly, as if
your dying could be a nicety.
As if you would hold the cup
to your mouth,walk around

the room like anyone. Later,
when the nurses came back
we sat at the foot of the bed
cupping your feet in our hands
watching them washing
you – peel away the gown
from your breasts. Your skin

was bluish now, Catherine
like the top of the sea at night.
The cave of your mouth
slowly darkening, filling –
the steps of your teeth
disappearing under the waves
of fluid   like sand.

TIM CUMMING
Margarine

You're incapable of the grand gesture
my father tells me from his hospital bed.
He's talking about the way I spread margarine.

His fingers play with the lead of a walkman
and it is a mystery to me how these small parts
of the world have swollen into my father's hands.

My feet beat a nervous tattoo
on the linoleum tiles of the hospital ward
and I wonder what has made him think of margarine,

the careful way I spread it on my toast,
and who, I ask, has ever spread margarine
to make it look like a grand gesture?

RUTH PADEL
Mary's First

She wants to leave me.
To continue as a white newt.
Tan-spotted, crested.
A large one. Handsome,
as newts go.

Her last human request
is to be pushed,
new gills pulsating,
into the orchestra pit
but racing green pondwater

sloshes from compartments
in her empty pram.
This holds me up and I lose her
under the seat of someone
unendingly angry.

We spot the screen
with our panicky silhouette
and some precision instrument
makes itself known
in my head, asking

What will you do now,
with the rest of your life,
plus the first bit,
that ended like this
in lost amphibia?

SHARON OLDS
The Lifting

Suddenly my father lifted up his nightie, I
turned my head away but he cried out
Shar!, my nickname, so I turned and looked.
He was sitting in the high cranked-up bed with the
gown up, around his neck,
to show me the weight he had lost. I looked
where his solid ruddy stomach had been
and I saw the skin fallen into loose
soft hairy rippled folds
lying in a pool of folds
down at the base of his abdomen,
the gaunt torso of a big man
who will die soon. Right away
I saw how much his hips are like mine,
the long, white angles, and then
how much his pelvis is shaped like my daughter's,
a chambered whelk-shell hollowed out,
I saw the folds of skin like something
poured, a thick batter, I saw
his rueful smile, the cast-up eyes as he
shows me his old body, he knows
I will be interested, he knows I will find him
appealing. If anyone had ever told me
I would sit by him and he would pull up his nightie
and I would look at him, at his naked body,
at the thick bud of his penis in all that
dark hair, look at him
in affection and uneasy wonder,
I would not have believed it. But now I can still
see the tiny snowflakes, white and
night-blue, on the cotton of the gown as it
rises the way we were promised at death it would rise,
the veils would fall from our eyes, we would know everything.

FRANCES HOROVITZ
Elegy

– No, we were not close
nor had we been for years.
Too great a harshness intervened,
accusation, anger.
'A clever daughter gone downhill' you said
– at best accustomed enemies
signalling hopefully
in a bleak landscape.

And now you weep before me.
With wasted arms you draw me down
till, legs strained,
I fear to fall onto your white bed.
Your pursed old-man's lips seek mine,
you say 'Forgive me'
and I cannot think for what

– nor what comfort I may give:
to talk to you of death
hopeless, an intrusion.
I do not know your faith, nor mine
nor what god you remember
from choirboy days,
your Sunday Christ
soon cut to size
by weekday rent unpaid.
I see you now in a sepia photograph
with other ragged boys –
the sharp pinched faces
of the thriving poor.

'Stay in your own corner,' you said,
'don't let them knock you down'...
Did you stay upright in your narrow life?
All I know is, by default
you taught your daughters how to glean for joy.

On high pillows your head lolls sideways,
flesh fallen from the bone,
eyelids half flicker open.

I see how like you
I shall become.

FRANCES WILSON
Endings

I wanted my mother to fight.
I wanted people to say, How splendid!
How indomitable – at ninety still loving
her grandchildren, her garden, The Guardian,
still dismissing slipshod thinking,
split infinitives. I wished she wouldn't
yield so easily, wouldn't stay upstairs
waiting to die, while downstairs
I'd listen to her tread from bed to window
to commode to bed, scraping thin skin
from new potatoes, staring into the murky water.

But I wanted my cat to go quietly,
to uncurl obediently from my lap, acquiesce
to the cat basket, to my right to save him
from suffering, myself from having to witness
his plucky, undignified failure to leap
onto the boiler; not summon up this
last ferocity, not fight, his old self,
ears flat, eyes wide, howl, scratch
all the way to the vet; to leave me
prising open tins with our faulty opener,
ears still half pricked for his silent arrival.

JOHN SMITH
Death at the Opera

Is this what death is like? I sit
Dressed elegantly in black and white, in an expensive seat.
Watching Violetta expire in Convent Garden.
How beautiful she is! As her voice lures me toward her death
The strings of the orchestra moisten my eyes with tears.
Though the tenor is too loud. Is this what death is like?
No one moves. Violetta coughs; stumbles toward the bed.
Twenty miles away in the country my father is dying.
Violetta catches at her throat. Let me repeat: my father
Is dying in a semi-detached house on a main road
Twenty miles off in the country. The skull is visible.

I do not want it to end. How exquisitely moving is death.
The approach to it. The lovers sob. Soon they will be wrenched
    apart.
How romantic it all is. Her hand is a white moth
Fluttering against the coverlet of the bed. The bones
Of my father's hands poke through his dry skin.
His eyes look into a vacancy of space. He spits into a cup.
In a few moments now Violetta will give up the ghost;
The doctor, the maid, the tenor who does not love her will sob.
Almost, our hearts will stop beating. How refreshed we have been.
My father's clothes, too large for his shrunken frame,
Make him look like a parcel. Ah! The plush curtains are opening.
The applause! The applause! It drowns out the ugly noise
Of my father's choking and spitting. The bright lights
Glitter far more than the hundred watt bulb at home.
Dear Violetta! How she enjoys flowers, like wreaths,
Showered for her own death. She gathers them to her.
We have avoided the coffin. I think that my father
Would like a box of good plain beech, being a man
From Buckinghamshire, a man of the country, a man of the soil.
I have seen my father, who is fond of animals, kill a cat
That was old and in pain with a blow from the edge of his palm.
He buried it in the garden, but I cannot remember its name.

Now the watchers are dispersing; the taxis drive away
Black in the black night. A huddle of people wait
Like mourners round the stage door. Is this what death is like?
For Violetta died after all. It is merely a ghost,
The voice gone, the beautiful dress removed, who steps in the rain.
Art, I conceive, is not so removed from life; for we look at death
Whether real or imagined, from an impossible distance
And somewhere a final curtain is always descending.
The critics are already phoning their obituaries to the papers.
I do not think God is concerned with such trivial matters
But, father, though there will be no applause, die well.

THOM GUNN
Still Life

I shall not soon forget
The greyish-yellow skin
To which the face had set:
Lids tight: nothing of his,
No tremor from within,
Played on the surfaces.

He still found breath, and yet
It was an obscure knack.
I shall not soon forget
The angle of his head,
Arrested and reared back
On the crisp field of bed,

Back from what he could neither
Accept, as one opposed,
Nor, as a life-long breather,
Consentingly let go,
The tube his mouth enclosed
In an astonished O.

PAUL HYLAND
A Proper Vanity

Her hair glistened in sunlight
and her hands, knotted and frail at rest,
unpinned it fluently, unloosed
the braided white, combed and caressed
the skein unfurling to her waist.

Miraculous that it should root
between a skull and skin pared
to a bare necessity, spared
this last grace. Her wasted face
fell into sensuous repose,

properly vain, till her grim hands
set to plait up each straying strand;
her glory, weight of womanhood
laboriously dressed, braided
and bound; its business, to persist.

FRANK ORMSBY
A Day in August

And still no stronger. Swathed in rugs he lingered
   Near to the windows, gauging distant hills.
Balked by the panes that promised light and flowers,
   The wasps were dying furiously on sills.

A doctor called. She walked him to the doorstep,
   Then sent the children out to gather cones
Under the trees beside the ruined churchyard.
   They romped, unheeding, in the tilted stones.

And now the wheels are turning. They impress
   Tracks that will not outlast the winter's rain.
The siren leaves a wash of emptiness.
   He is lost to the small farms, lane by lane.

STAN SMITH
Deathbed

Feeling, at this centre
gills throb, suck
of the hours like water

the mind opening, shutting
– sifted: expelled –
Staring at the ceiling

cod's eyes transfix
the stretched daylight:
there are only the bricks

rigid, passionless,
the white plaster;
on the stairs, voices.

It all in the end runs back
to this single room,
these few hours, this cul-de-sac.

Nothing confers. Nothing
is diminished. Ice walls
hold the evening.

DUNCAN CURRY
September 15th, 1989

The room is a collapsing lung.
I fan you with a towel, red and yellow gill.

We fiddle with sheets, window blinds,
small jobs to lend helplessness a purpose.

The ward is quieter now. Across the garden, willow hangs
and a Tree of Heaven burns brown in late sun.

You awaken and all the life left
focuses in your left eye, blue,

like a bulb about to break
which grows suddenly brighter.

RON BUTLIN
from **Ryecroft**
(in memory of my mother who died 4th November 1991)

1 *Departures*

My mother died much slower than expected:
I saw her, talked, held her hands, sat,
held her hands, kissed goodbye
and left the nursing home. That visit lasted seven months.

Soon it will be March. We have returned to work on Ryecroft:
a front door of hardwood panels crumbling
to yellow dampness;
a backdoor of corrugated metal hammered
onto rotten planks.
The window frames and ceilings are secured by clouded stillness
gathered into filth around the bundled-up dead.
Uncurtained daylight chills me.

There has been no winter until now:
it is a room already hardened into ice around
a hairbrush, comb, kleenex, photographs and her
stiffening face upon the pillow.

KEN SMITH
Milly's End

She died. Worse was her undoing,
the tongue's unravelling, the memory's flat battery

coughing in the night *someone has taken my orange juice,*
someone has stolen my shoes. Up,

down, either was difficult, *it's not*
her any more I hear my voice say again

through the narrowing months of her vision
that could see bright clear to a winter day.

There was a war, she worked in the harvest
of wet beets, soldiers came in and out her gate,

in and out of her kitchen, hot white mugs
in their hard cold hands.

Where are they all now? she asks.
How many ever came back?

GEORGE MacBETH
On the Death of May Street
(for my grandfather)

You built it, and baptised it with her name,
Sixty-eight years ago. No angel came

The first Edwardian day to plant the stone
And make a child. Your wife conceived alone

And bore my mother in that soaking room
Where water later flowed, that choked her womb.

Tonight I write that May Street is condemned
And sure to die, as she was. Gripped and hemmed

By the sour blood of change, that rips and kills,
It dies far quicker than she did by pills.

I own it, and I see it broken, stone
By mother-naked stone. I heard her groan

That last night in our house before she died,
Not knowing how to help her. So I cried,

As I do now inside, to see her name
Shaken, and wasted. For your wasted fame

I cry to you, grandfather, in your grave
In rage and grief. All that you failed to save

Has shrunk to geometry, to crumbled lime
Beside the brickworks, to your grandson's rhyme.

JAMES WRIGHT
An Elegy for the Poet Morgan Blum

Morgan the lonely,
Morgan the dead,
Has followed his only
Child into a vast
Desolation.
When I heard he was going
I tried to blossom
Into the boat beside him,
But I had no money.

When I went to see him,
The nurse said no.
So I snuck in behind her.
And there they were.

They were there, for a moment.
Red Jacket, Robert Hayman,
H. Phelps Putnam,
And sweet Ted Roethke,
A canary and a bear.

They looked me over,
More or less alive.
They looked at me, more
Or less out of place.
They said, get out,
Morgan is dying.
They said, get out,
Leave him alone.

We have no kings
In this country,
They kept saying.
But we have one
Where the dead rise
On the other shore.
And they hear only
The cold owls throwing
Salt over
Their secret shoulders.

So I left Morgan,
And all of them alone.
And now I am so lonely
For the air I want to breathe.
Come breathe me, dark prince.
And Morgan lay there
Clean shaved like a baby
By the nurse who said no.
And so a couple
Of years ago,
The old poets died
Young.

And now the young,
Scarlet on their wings, fly away
Over the marshes.

PAUL DURCAN
Glocca Morra

Dear Daughter – Watching my father die,
As one day you will watch me die,
In the public ward of a centre-city hospital,
Mid-afternoon bustle,
A transistor radio playing two or three beds away,
Paintwork flaking on the wall,
His breath dwindling,
His throat gurgling,
A source disappearing slowly,
Source of all that I am before my eyes evaporating,
Well, watching your own father die slowly in front of you,
Die slowly right under your nose,
Is a bit like sitting in the front row of the concert hall
Watching a maestro performing Tchaikovsky's Grand Piano Sonata.
It's spectacular, so to speak,
But the audience feels helpless.

When Daddy died
I wrung my hands at the foot of his bed
Until a consultant doctor told me to stop it
And to show some respect for the dead.
The old prick.
He had done nothing for Daddy
Except pollute him with pills for twenty years
For fees in guineas.
They threw a sheet over him
And put screens around the bed
But I stood my ground
At the foot of the bed
While the transistor radio,
Like something hidden in a hedgerow,
Went on with its programme –
Rosemary Clooney crooning
'How are Things in Glocca Morra?'

Outside the ward window
– Which was in need of cleaning, I noticed –
The sun was going down in the west over the Phoenix Park

Where Daddy and me
('Daddy and I' – he corrects me –
He was a stickler for grammar),
Where Daddy and I
Played all sorts of games for years,
Football, hurling, cricket, golf, donkey,
Before he got into his Abraham-and-Isaac phase
And I got the boat to England
Before he had time to chop off my head.

O Daddy dear –
As we find ourselves alone together for the last time,
Marooned in this centre-city hospital public ward,
I think that there is something consoling-cheerful, even –
About the transistor playing away in the next bed.
The day you bought your first transistor
You took us out for a drive in the car,
The Vauxhall Viva,
Down to a derelict hotel by the sea,
The Glocca Morra,
Roofless, windowless, silent,
And, you used add with a chuckle,
Scandalous.
You dandled it on your knee
And you stated how marvellous a gadget it was,
A portable transistor,
And that you did not have to pay
A licence fee for it,
You chuckled.
A man not much known for chuckling.
The Glocca Morra,
Roofless, windowless, silent and *scandalous.*

Rosemary Clooney –
The tears are lumbering down my cheeks, Dad –
She must be about the same age as you,
Even looks like you.
I bet her handwriting
Is much the same as yours.
You had a lovely hand,
Cursive, flourishing, exuberant, grateful, actual, generous.
Whatever things are like in Glocca Morra
I'm sad that we're not going to be together any more.

Dear Daughter – If and when the time comes
For you to watch me die,
In a public place to watch me
Trickling away from you,
Consider the paintwork on the wall
And check out the music in the next bed.
'How are Things in Glocca Morra?'
Every bit as bad as you might think they are –
Or as good. Or not so bad. Love, Dad.

SEAMUS HEANEY
from **Clearances**

3

When all the others were away at Mass
I was all hers as we peeled potatoes.
They broke the silence, let fall one by one
Like solder weeping off the soldering iron:
Cold comforts set between us, things to share
Gleaming in a bucket of clean water.
And again let fall. Little pleasant splashes
From each other's work would bring us to our senses.

So while the parish priest at her bedside
Went hammer and tongs at the prayers for the dying
And some were responding and some crying
I remembered her head bent towards my head,
Her breath in mine, our fluent dipping knives –
Never closer the whole rest of our lives.

7

In the last minutes he said more to her
Almost than in all their life together.
'You'll be in New Row on Monday night
And I'll come up for you and you'll be glad
When I walk in the door... Isn't that right?'
His head was bent down to her propped-up head.
She could not hear but we were overjoyed.

He called her good and girl. Then she was dead,
The searching for a pulsebeat was abandoned
And we all knew one thing by being there.
The space we stood around had been emptied
Into us to keep, it penetrated
Clearances that suddenly stood open.
High cries were felled and a pure change happened.

GLYN HUGHES
Old Man

Until the end of sunset, the great chestnut tree
clutched a ray of light to its heart
and the old man always sat under it, as if he felt
that holding a light within the surrounding dark
was a symbol of the proper way to depart.

ANDREW MOTION
Postscript

Next door my father lay in his vacant bed.
Beyond fifteen miles of snow his wife
Sweated in the ward's cacophony
And could not sleep.

I heard him start to snore, until,
Headlong on a dream, the world sank;
I awoke to daylight,
'Mother' like a last star on my tongue.

II. A few minutes after my father dies...

TIM CUMMING
The Balcony

A few minutes after my father dies
a doctor from the night shift enters
to confirm his death. He's dead, and we walk
onto the balcony of the patient's television room
where it is quiet, and watch the ferry from Boulogne
dock into the harbour of the town.
My brother says something.
I don't know what he does with his hands.
We don't know what to do with ourselves.
Back home, my father's pills
fill the cupboard above the boiler,
and his glasses on a shelf above the sink.
Paper with his writing on it,
written two or three years earlier.
Hair in an electric shaver.
The remains of a hurried lunch, and ground coffee.
When the priest is called
he comes with the obedience of his calling.
We take an elevator, and find the car
by automatic reflex.
It rains several times. I don't sleep.

Beer

I was drinking
the evening my father died.
I sat outside my brother's house
and drank beers with him
and a friend of his
from across the road
and when it began to rain
at one or two in the morning
I put on my jacket
and opened another can.

A few nights ago
at Poole general hospital
my brother and I
sat by our father's bed
and when we got up to go
we said we'd go and have a few drinks,
and we had a few beers,
and we've been drinking,
and now we're drunk,

and when I hear
someone banging the shit
out of the grain silo
on Damory Down
where my brother lives,
where the edge of the town
is edged with cars
and the parts of cars,
it sounds to me like my father.

It's one or two in the morning,
and we're all cried out,
we've shaken out our father
like shaking out dust from an old blanket.
The wind is up,
and I walk backwards into the house,
and from the house to the hospital,
the hospital to the train,
and the train to the station.
The air smells of cigarettes
and the Badger brewery by the river
on the other side of the town.
I break open a bottle
and wait for a call.
On the edge of town,
the banging starts again.

JOHN STONE
Death

I have seen   come on
slowly as rust
sand

or suddenly   as when
someone leaving a room

finds the doorknob
come loose in his hand

JOHN HARTLEY WILLIAMS
The Awful Ignominy of My Father's Death

We put him on the bed & he groaned.
We called the doctor on our tin-can telephone.
The doctor seemed to be counting haystacks in his mind.
Then the ambulance came,
A Gryphon & a Hoarse Hat Wearer.
They had a stretcher like a corridor.
My mother said: 'All the time I've known him
He's never done anything like that before.'
How long had she known him, after all?
Not a man for the ladies really,
More a man for the well-chosen word.
They took away his education, left only
Priceless, urine-steeped volumes
Under the bed.

That was that really.
In the hospital at Steglitz
He had a half-jointed grin,
The other half had fallen down a hole in his trouser leg.
A lady folded him into all kinds of shapes.

He slopped backwards & forwards like a highly intelligent pancake,
He was a thumb that had lost the route to its mouth.
She was obviously highly-trained.
Where did you get this training, I wanted to say:
The Florida Everglades?
Flamingoes write hate letters to Walt Disney, you know!
The expertise of her doing good was
A warning light on the jetliner before it crashes.
I mumbled:
Put him back in the drink & call the Royal Air Force!

Just before my Dad had his crow-like discomfiture with the branch
        he was sitting on,
He & I had had a bit of an argument about the nature of the tree,
Whether it was a Birch or an Oak or an alabaster mock-up of a Baobab.
Now his mouth was propped open with a darning mushroom,
The part of him that hadn't been poleaxed by a mad aardvark
Was saying: 'Just let me out of this flesh-prison
And I'll put these people straight on matters pertaining to everything!'
It was disgusting. I was the monotonous person
Who wd soon drive home by myself.
He wd fly back horizontally to the place he had last been vertical in.

I only saw him once more alive. They were teaching him to read.
Gigantic seagulls were walking all over the grey beach of his belly,
Laying eggs in the hairy cleft of his thighs.
'I've already done this,' he said, closing the book.
The nurses had kid-glove eyes.
They were the kind that wd have asked Julius Caesar if he was
        feeling better now.
I thought suddenly we'd gone on an excursion,
As if one of those old steam trains had puffed into a wood,
And the carriage door opened & everybody got out,
And it was summer,
So we said 'What a wonderful place for a party!'
Opened our hampers & popped the champagne corks,
Raised our glasses and sang 'Never trust a man who doesn't drink!'
Meanwhile my father struggled to voice a reprimand:
'Never trust a man who does!'
Which we couldn't hear, him being inaudible & so on.

And then we threw the empty glasses into the trees,
And I said 'Cheerio!' I'd see him in a month or so,
We'd talk then, even tho I knew
The railway was due for closure, no way of getting back,
And soon they'd build a supermarket
Just where his bed
Grew shady in the leaves.

The last time I saw my father
He had shrunk to the size of a matchbox.
He was very neat & pale.
He was singing *The Teddy Bear's Picnic* under his breath.
The undertaker was a very practical man:
He carried a spade, some rosewater, a pack of playing cards (all aces)
        & a car battery.
He kept saying things like:

**All You Have To Do
Is Decide
What Not To Write On The Stone**

Then he put the jump leads on my father's toes.

SHIRLEY GEOK-LIN LIM
Anna's Faith

A foot of fresh snow arrived today,
a foot of white with no grey or yellow
in it. You would have been eighty today.
Other birthdays rejoice this morning.

Some years brought blue crocus,
fisted hyacinths, narcissi early forming.
Today brought snow you would have murmured
at. Your home was musty, clean, smelling

of soap chips, like you after years of rinsing.
Catholic, bent small and propped on pillows,
a baby labouring for breath, you viewed
the park's grey lichen without a shadow

of irony, pressing your childless palm, light
as a page, on my sleeve. One would want to pretend
for you more love than one had; to be good outside
one's self, condescension at your pliant faith

in weak tea and crochet squares muted through
your dying to something else, perhaps,
better; for once, late in the evening,
kissing the papery cheek goodbye, true.

TONY HARRISON
Flood

His home address was inked inside his cap
and on every piece of paper that he carried
even across the church porch of the snap
that showed him with mi mam just minutes married.

But if ah'm found at 'ome (he meant found dead)
turn t'water off. Through his last years he nursed,
more than a fear of dying, a deep dread
of his last bath running over, or a burst.

Each night towards the end he'd pull the flush
then wash, then in pyjamas, rain or snow,
go outside, kneel down in the yard, and push
the stopcock as far off as it would go.

For though hoping that he'd drop off in his sleep
he was most afraid, I think, of not being 'found'
there in their house, his ark, on firm Leeds ground
but somewhere that kept moving, cold, dark, deep.

JANET FISHER
C.W.G.

In the guest house convenient for the hospital
by the window overlooking the playing field,
my clothes on the twin bed next to the radiator
and the painted doorstop in the shape of a reindeer,

I lie cramped up because of something I've eaten,
watching Benny and Ronnie on UK Gold.
I can't find the off switch. Four gobs of bird shit,
three men with hoses. I rush for the sink.

Before the fall he lived by himself,
did his own cooking. Moved slowly.
An hour for breakfast. An hour and a half
to bathe and dress. Shaved from memory.

His fingers angrily search the sheets.
His voice cracks. He gives me orders.
I buy him the *Telegraph*. Cheats, waste, lies.
'How do they manage to keep clean?'

The death certificate says broncho-pneumonia.
The cremation is nothing, twenty minutes,
a selection from *Patience*, no hymns.
Something in my stomach like a pain.

KATHARINE MIDDLETON
Her Death

Her death, and the soot-blackened hospital wall
ten minutes behind him,
he comes down the deserted road
to the bus-stop where no one's waiting.

The concrete shelter is roofed and open-fronted;
shaped, he's thought often these last few weeks,
like a pavilion for spectators
at a tournament, at games.

Now it flies great flags – night's navy-blue,
white pennons of the bleak street-lights,
and the colourless, all-coloured
flags of chaos.

At the edge of the world
he stands looking out on the mists of space.
Out there the arena, the tiers of seats,
lie empty.

The bus from Andromeda arrives.
The return-half of his ticket will take him
somewhere, even though the place he set out from
will no longer be there.

PATRICIA BISHOP
Child with Liver Damage

I had "specialed" him,
coming in when off duty
with the odd comic, a bar of chocolate.
He would lie with his eyes closed
but twitching a little
like a snared rabbit.
His hands soft with disuse.

Even his hair slipped away
so each day we'd find
brown threads on the pillow.
All this so long ago
I forget his name even.
In the end he could only sip
from a feeding spout.

When it happened
I told the parents.
She had an odd little hat
skew-whiff over her forehead.
The knot of his tie
too small, too tight,
like their hands.
'Thank you nurse,' they said,
as if I had told them the time.

SHARON OLDS
The Exact Moment of His Death

When he breathed his last breath, it was he,
my father, although he was so transformed
no one who had not been with him
for the last hour would know him – the skin
now physical as animal fat,
the eyes cast halfway back into his head,
the nose thinned, the mouth racked open,
with that tongue in it like the fact of the mortal,
a tongue so dried, scalloped, darkened
and material. We could see the fluid
risen into the back of his mouth
but it was he, the huge, slack arms,
the spots of blood under the skin
black and precise, we had come this far with him
step by step, it was he, his last
breath was his, not taken with desire
but his, light as a milkweed seed,
coming out of his mouth and floating across the room.
And-when the nurse listened for his heart;
and his stomach was silvery, it was his stomach,
when she did not shake her head but stood and
nodded at me, for a moment it was fully
he, my father, dead but completely
himself, a man with an open mouth and
black spots on his arms. He looked like

someone killed in a bloodless struggle –
the strain in his neck and the base of his head,
as if he were violently pulling back.
He seemed to be holding still, then the skin
tightened slightly around his whole body
as if the purely physical were claiming him,
and then it was not my father,
it was not a man, it was not an animal,
I ran my hand slowly through the hair,
lifted my fingers up through the grey
waves of it, the unliving glistening
matter of this world.

IAN McDONALD
Walking in the Stars

Last words are not remarkable as a rule.
They drift away, have nothing much to say,
Murmurs hardly loud enough to catch the ear:
'Please for some water', 'I so cold in here'.
Not more nor less than this or that.
Dying is a puzzled, incoherent act.
But this one! He described his desert days,
Rose-coloured forts and old battalion pals.
'Servant of the Crown', one of the old school,
He served the King in post-war Palestine.

One still, clear night in Galilee
The stars dripped silver in a midnight sea.
He and his platoon went wading out
Far from shore so that they could shout
Loud among the stars and be heard by God.
He ends before he ends the story:
A sentence cut in half is his last word.
His exultant voice clamours to be heard:
'I, walking in the stars, in great glory...'

RON BUTLIN
from **Ryecroft**
(in memory of my mother who died 4th November 1991)

7 *The curtains were closed*

The curtains were closed when I entered your room:
the day was shut out, the night was shut out
and you weren't there.

I looked down at your face, your mouth and your eyes:
I tried to remember your mouth and your eyes.

The walls were as mist when mist disappears;
the door falling rain that no longer falls –

the corridor ran the length of the world
and you weren't there.

OKTAY RIFAT
Lament
(translated from the Turkish by Ruth Christie)

First your outer covering wore away,
your flesh, your eyes and eyebrows wore away.
Whatever you knew as fresh and young, burned out,
                                            burned out.

Hand and foot you lost my friend,
Pen-slim finger and nail.
Life and spirit were yours,
                    now lost and gone,
What's left of you, my friend, reduced
                            to lines in books.
– Where lashes, hair and skin?

Oh shoddy world!
– But once an Orhan Veli lived.
Come, brother Orhan, come,

                              Take my hands,
                              Use my eyes.

MAURA DOOLEY
Gone

You were only a bag of soft stuff
but I imagined you like a nut,
your brain beginning to pack itself
around the kernel that was me.
My limpet, my leech,
my little sucker-in of blood.
Gone. Sometimes I think we know
of nothing else, lost loves, lost lives,
the hopeless benediction of rain.

IMOGEN MONEY
After Two Months

My grandmother is dying of leukaemia.
Mother phoned to tell me.
My exams begin tomorrow.
They won't let me go
to say goodbye to her.
I think the revision has gone well;
Grey squirrel,
Brown levret,
Dandelion ducklings.

My grandmother died today.
It was grandfather's birthday,
They read poetry.
I think my exam was OK;
Was spared the aftermath and postmortems.
I sat on the walls of a Gothic castle.
Eating chips with chili-sauce.
Each morsel fried,
Dripping red
Matching her last beats.
Her struggle for breath.

My grandmother died.
They postponed the funeral
While I sat exams.
When I arrived everybody was ready.
The flowers had been ordered.
I would have chosen freesias,
Cornflowers by the bucket
Gypsophilia snowing down,
I wanted to say goodbye,
But death, they were worried,
Could be a cheat.

MARINA AMA OMOWALE MAXWELL
To My Grandmother, Lady-Woman

I wasn't there
when you died
when they laid you out
                    as you had lived, a little starchy

stiffly
from your middle parted hair, old bun
resting
to your bunioned feet.

I wasn't there
when they stopped you,
                    as you had lived, ever moving on

Walking, walking, ever walking
to feed poor children
giving them their break/
fast
shed
with your coterie of tears.

But I remember,
a firm dignity of wrinkles
brown-lined face
and thinking, thinking, ever thinking eyes.

I remember,
your endless scholarships for poor girls
and boys
giving them their break/
fast
with your black leather encased bunioned feet
worn shoes, walking
shaped to the bunions of your pain.

It is your brown song you poured into my mother's face
your strength
that kept her back straight up
as she too
Red Crossed the white world, our melee world
Head high
Her tiny feet treading paths unknown
for women
then.

It is your bundled self
with your great sloping shoulders
that you gave to her
and passed
into my song.

IF I CARRY BANNERS
THEN AND NOW
IT IS YOUR SONG
AND HERS
THAT I SALUTE

DAVID CONSTANTINE
from In Memoriam 8571 Private J.W. Gleave,
who was at Montauban, Trônes Wood and Guillemont

'So many without memento...'

3 *Notification*

It was the painful duty of Lieutenant Thomas Dinsdale
On Army Form B 104-82
In an envelope the postwoman shrank from touching
To notify my grandmother of her altered state.
The women stood by, they followed the post like crows:
To whom would such a communication come
That morning, to what woman by the hand of a woman
Whose job it was daily to visit that village of streets
And lay the stigmata on certain doors?

So the news came from Guillemont to Salford 5
After a lapse of weeks during which time
She had known no better than to believe herself a wife.

7

There being no grave, there being not even one
Ranked among millions somewhere in France,
Her grief went without where to lay its head.
She would have rested sooner had she had
Or had she even learned somewhere there was
A well-kept place where he was lying dead.

She could not even think him out of harm:
He must be hurt somewhere by every shell,
Somewhere his mouth could not get breath for gas.
She would have scavenged all his body home
Into the shelter of if not her house
At least the roofed and hidden well-walled grave.

But of what comfort is the body home
Which here or there cannot embrace or smile?
And of what comfort is the body whole?
Only the rich and saints do not corrupt.
She almost thought there were degrees of death
And he was more dead piecemeal and abroad.

There being nowhere but the family grave
She went and called her grief out of the air
And coaxed it to alight upon the stone
That did not bear his name. Upon that absence
She grieved as though it were the greater one
And death was lured almost within her view.

She set that feature on the featureless
Visibly everlasting plain of death
She trod a path, she made some little inroad
And placing three or four remembrance days
She netted in their few interstices
Glimpses that she could bear out of the deep.

* * *

9 *Like shrapnel*

Like shrapnel in the lucky ones
She carried fragments in her speech
Remarkable to grandchildren
But to herself accustomed
Like rise and shine and left
Left...he had a good home and he left
And a long, long trail a-winding...

JOHN FIGUEROA
Epitaph

The old man is gone
        Him ded, sah, him ded!
(Where are the frigate birds?)

Absent from Jonkunoo Lounge,
Someone will miss him from
The Caribe Bar – but only long
After.
        Him ded, sah, him ded!

In Santiago de los Caballeros
(O Spanish men on horses!)
They will remember when
It is too late how lively he
Could be.
        Him ded, sah; se murio.
But Tavern on the Green
Will dance, and Tower Isle
And Myrtle Bank, so stupidly
Demolished.
        (Him done ded, sah)
And wherever for a moment or
A night he used to cast the spell
Against death with dancing –
A spell that works and does
Not work.
        (Him ded, sah, him ded!)
A spell that did not last.

The frigate birds have soared away.
The hurricane clouds have left
The skies clean blue;
And in the silence he has danced
Away, away, across the bar.

        Him no ded, sah?

PATRICIA BEER
The Lost Woman

My mother went with no more warning
Than a bright voice and a bad pain.
Home from school on a June morning
And where the brook goes under the lane
I saw the back of a shocking white
Ambulance drawing away from the gate.

She never returned and I never saw
Her buried. So a romance began.
The ivy-mother turned into a tree
That still hops away like a rainbow down
The avenue as I approach.
My tendrils are the ones that clutch.

I made a life for her over the years.
Frustrated no more by a dull marriage
She ran a canteen through several wars.
The wit of a cliché-ridden village
She met her match at an extra-mural
Class and the OU summer school.

Many a hero in his time
And every poet has acquired
A lost woman to haunt the home,
To be compensated and desired,
Who will not alter, who will not grow,
A corpse they need never get to know.

She is nearly always benign. Her habit
Is not to stride at dead of night.
Soft and crepuscular in rabbit-
Light she comes out. Hear how they hate
Themselves for losing her as they did.
Her country is bland and she does not chide.

But my lost woman evermore snaps
From somewhere else: 'You did not love me.
I sacrificed too much perhaps,
I showed you the way to rise above me
And you took it. You are the ghost
With the bat-voice, my dear. *I* am not lost.'

BRUCE DAWE
Going
(for my mother-in-law, Gladys)

Mum, you would have loved the way you went!
One moment, at a barbecue in the garden
– the next, falling out of your chair,
hamburger in one hand,
and a grandson yelling.

Zipp! The heart's roller blind
rattling up, and you, in an old dress,
quite still, flown already from your dearly-loved
Lyndon, leaving only a bruise like a blue kiss
on the side of your face, the seed-beds incredibly tidy,
grass daunted by drought.

You'd have loved it, Mum, you big spender! The relatives,
eyes narrowed with grief, swelling the rooms
with their clumsiness, the reverberations of tears, the endless
cuppas and groups revolving blinded as moths.

The joy of your going! The laughing reminiscences
snagged on the pruned roses
in the bright blowing day!

STEPHEN PARR
Passing Place

Butter
flies in mid
October,

wasps full of sleep
crawl
over the burning quilt

of leaves.
You've been dead
two days.

Already a small spider
has built his net
from rim

to handle
of your white enamel
shaving mug

JANE DURAN
I Have Thought

I have thought
of all the things
I could have done
for you, crowding
the way unspoken sentences
crowd in the shining gullet,
or boxcars string out
along a railway track
in some byway of the earth,
some heartbreaking noon
of long grass,
or shhh-ing as only shells
know how to shhh
when there is no more life in them.
So many quiet and dutiful things
I could have accomplished for you:
the way the walls of the Seine
bind back the city,
holding it away
or the carpentry of stars
hoists a forest at night
and whole towns.
I imagine that I might have made
the weeks of your dying easier,
though you were breathing
your last breaths,
and stood with you head bowed
very near to your death,
beside your own self.
Perhaps then I would have been
no more than a pale scarf
just seen through the olive trees
or a banner of wind,
burning with sea
burning with the certain world,
far in the distance
far from the hurricane you were in.

MARION LOMAX
Transliteration
(for Ann)

Twenty years ago at the moment my father died
I was trying to transliterate заканчивать,
had substituted more than half of it: ZAKANCHIV...
in capitals on top of a three-by-four buff card.
Like most things I did in those days, it made little sense.
I followed instructions; behaved as was expected –
filed Russian cards, drove north each weekend, watched him suffer
for two years while no one acknowledged he was dying –
wanted to risk truth but didn't dare to. Daily we
dragged an unspeakable secret around with our souls.
Then, the most apt word would have been страшный:
for him, for us, there was no sign of it finishing.

In those days, at work, my eyes read all words as Russian
whatever the language – so that today, when I hear
Mandelstam's poetry read by a woman whose name
I cannot catch, my mind lurches from the moon, a clock,
the clapping, crowded room, to the desk where I waited
every Friday afternoon before the long haul home,
desperate to translate the incomprehensible
into something which would allow me to bring comfort
to him, my mother, myself. Yet transliteration
was all that was asked of me – just the substitution
of sham for true letters – to form words we could handle,
but nothing that might ever make a living language.

ALISON FELL
Border Raids
(for my grandmother)

Fierce pins plough her hair
You can tell by the angry drag
of the net
that once she was beautiful,
envied and glad of it
The nightingale of the county,
electrifying the village halls

She told me she wore winged hats
tall as gladioli,
and the hanging moon sang with her,
and how they clapped and horded
at her doors

When she went,
she went like the old bunch, cursing,
blue as smoke,
you could almost smell the burning
(Oh, they were a wild lot, the Johnstones,
border raiders,
horse stealers, setting the Kirk alight
and all their enemies inside)

With her heart tattered
as a tyre on the road
she begged for morphine
and to be done with it,
to be gone among the gliding dead

She glints now in the gooseberry bushes,
her broom hisses out at low-dashing cats
In the night she slaps up her window
and hurls hairbrushes

I've been thinking
If I could go back,
stealing up the cemetery hill
to borrow back her bones,
I'd give her to the merry gods
of the midsummer garden
who dance among the columbines
who fib and fart
and I'd tell them to trumpet her out

MAGGIE BEVAN
'Gag'
(for my gran, Jenny May Hawkins Brooke, died aged 94)

1 *Touch*

Violet talcum clogs the air.
It's us, Gag. It's us.
White-haired, lost in the pillow
she doesn't know, can't connect.
It's us. Her wiry eyebrows twitch:
Don't leave me, she mouthes,
then – *When will I die?*
Soon, we say as she slips back
below the surface of words
to that lonely place
where her body's against her.
We hold hands in silence.

All that's left is touch.

2 *Gone*

Jenny May Hawkins Brooke. Gone.
May Brooke. May Jarman. Gone.
Gran. Gan. Gag. Gone.
The word, final as a thump.

3 3rd March, 1990

Don't ever get old. I'm dressing her.
You never think it'll come to this.
Holding her hands. Hands

she was proud of and tended like roses.
Nails now, picked to the quick,
You never think. Gag, almost blind.

One by one I fetched her plants.
With seeing fingers she stroked
each upturned face. Her children.

4 *Her Hands*

Gag's in her room lipreading the telly,
hands twisting invisible threads
in her lap. Suddenly,
I'm a kid again at her feet,
entranced, as plump and long-nailed,
her hands knit me back into the past.

Her hands worked while Arth disappeared
for days, carting camera and sacks
off to the hills and his eagles.
They sorted and sold in the shop –
evenings would knit and crochet
through orders for well-heeled folk.

Her hands didn't stop. Twenty years
after Arth's death they went on hunting wool
at jumbles, unpicking, washing, winding
crinkled colours round chair-backs;
transforming the past into mittens,
jumpers, scarves, good as new, for us.

Thirty years. And still crocheting –
neat, fast as a spider –
chairbacks to defend against
the grease of men's hair,
doilies, teacosies, hankie trims...
Till her eyes for fine work dimmed.

Then she'd knit squares
with endless patience, join them
in quilts, vibrant gardens crammed
with haphazard shade and tone.
I always felt an order, a safety,
in her casual geometry of colour.

See her hands. Always moving.
But they slowed, grew bony and thin
as silk, veins sewn on in blue,
thick as the wool she'd worked with.
Her hands grew thinner, thinner till
one day her wedding ring fell off.

5 *Funeral Parlour*

The room's a fridge. Disinfected silence,
cut flowers, speak of order, lack of love.

I tread the soundless carpet to a coffin.
In it: a body. Mouth without mischief,

stuffed, altered. Forehead ironed free
of frowns above a skewiff nose. And under

the folds of a stiff sugar-pink dress
she'd have scoffed at: her hands.

Hidden. For age, for ugly maps of veins.
I take them out – her chill yellow hands.

Hold them, kiss the blue nails.
Hidden. Like so much. Like death.

I draw up a chair. Tell her what she knew:
We love you, over and over.

6 *Funeral*

They're going to burn you.
Us in Sunday best.
Crying. Flowers. Holding hands.

Thick organ music. Talcum.
Electronic curtains
close round the coffin.

They're going to burn you.
We waved you off
with suitcase and pluck
on countless jaunts with Darby & Joan.
Switzerland, even.
And you in your eighties.
We stayed on the tarmac waving
till your first jet was a toy.
You always came back.

They're going to burn you.
Now it's over.
The vicar laughing.
All shake hands.
We come out into daylight.
So hot it scalds.

KIT WRIGHT
Pub Death

All the ungrieving rain in heaven laced the sky
The pale day Rita came to die,

Fixing the lunch trade with an important look,
A swollen silence and a scotch for old time's sake

Which we sat and we drank. Upstairs
The silence became her mind. This took four years

We recalled, from her first being brought to bed
To the last drunk's last drink with the dead dead.

JOHN BETJEMAN
Death in Leamington

She died in the upstairs bedroom
   By the light of the ev'ning star
That shone through the plate glass window
   From over Leamington Spa.

Beside her the lonely crochet
   Lay patiently and unstirred,
But the fingers that would have work'd it
   Were dead as the spoken word.

And Nurse came in with the tea-things
   Breast high 'mid the stands and chairs –
But Nurse was alone with her own little soul,
   And the things were alone with theirs.

She bolted the big round window,
   She let the blinds unroll,
She set a match to the mantle,
   She covered the fire with coal.

And 'Tea!' she said in a tiny voice
   'Wake up! It's nearly *five*.'
Oh! Chintzy, chintzy cheeriness,
   Half dead and half alive!

Do you know that the stucco is peeling?
   Do you know that the heart will stop?
From those yellow Italianate arches
   Do you hear the plaster drop?

Nurse looked at the silent bedstead,
   At the gray, decaying face,
As the calm of a Leamington ev'ning
   Drifted into the place.

She moved the table of bottles
   Away from the bed to the wall,
And tiptoeing gently over the stairs
   Turned down the gas in the hall.

D.J. ENRIGHT
On the Death of a Child

The greatest griefs shall find themselves
        inside the smallest cage.
It's only then that we can hope to tame
        their rage,

The monsters we must live with. For it
        will not do
To hiss humanity because one human threw
Us out of heart and home. Or part

At odds with life because one baby failed
        to live.
Indeed, as little as its subject, is
        the wreath we give –

The big words fail to fit. Like giant boxes
Round small bodies. Taking up improper room,
Where so much withering is, and so much bloom.

DIANA SCOTT
Prayer for the Little Daughter Between Death and Burial

Now you are standing face to face with the clear light
believe in it
Now you have gone back into where air comes from
hold fast to it
Now you have climbed to the top of the topless tower
and there are no stairs down
and the only way is flight past the edge of the world
do not remember us

Like the new moon in the sky of the shortest day
you came to us
as the candles burnt with a steady light behind misty windows
you whispered to us
as the singers moved behind doors of un-attainable rooms
you burst in on us
Lady of the shortest day, silent upon the threshold
carrying green branches

Lady of the crown of light going into clear light
be safe on your journey
Bright lady of the dark day, who pushed back the darkness
say nothing to us
as we plod through the frozen field
going from somewhere to somewhere
do not speak to us
as we stand at the centre of the frozen lake
and trees of cloud stand over us
forget us

When we come to you we shall find you
who have seen Persephone
you whom our mothers called Lady of the city
will welcome us with tapers, and believe in us
When small harsh birds bubble and pump in our nude trees
and water will rush and gush through the slippery street
and two skies will look at each other
one of air and one below
of water
you will rest with us, and of us:

Lady of the shortest day
watch over our daughter
whom we commit to the grass

X.J. KENNEDY
Little Elegy
(for a child who skipped rope)

Here lies resting, out of breath,
Out of turns, Elizabeth
Whose quicksilver toes not quite
Cleared the whirring edge of night.

Earth whose circles round us skim
Till they catch the lightest limb,
Shelter now Elizabeth
And for her sake trip up death.

COLIN ROWBOTHAM
September

Horsechestnuts crushed on the road. My tiny son,
So lately born, dies in his pram – like that –
At a Harvest Supper. At home, alone,
I cradle the phone on Maggie's camouflaged
Message of death; reach hospital to learn
What I know already. We cling together, one
In grief. John's nodding body, limp
As a newborn's, cool flesh a bloodless tone
Of ivory. We kiss the pursed mouth, turn
Into a life as horizonless and flat

As an icefield. Despair is a shambling thing
In down-at-heel slippers, in a maze
Of corridors; an idiot lurching beast,
Steered at the elbow by friends from room to room:
Coroner, registrar – scrawling its dumb
Name to a typewriter's clatter; encountering
Joy's mirror image at each turn.
The death certificate is signed. Released
From red-tape, we rethread our route in numb
Silence, down echoing antiseptic ways

To autumn's hanging damp. A pride of slack
Giraffe-necked planetrees, arched in from the walls
Of the hospital courtyard, interweaves
Its variegating canopy above
A fountain-speckled pool that brims the stone
Lip of its basin. Locked in a desert of black
Asphalt mottled with the green
Litter of prematurely scattered leaves;
Discoursing through the motions of its own
Self-contained cycle – it gathers, rises, falls.

LUCILLE CLIFTON
The Lost Baby Poem

the time i dropped your almost body down
down to meet the waters under the city
and run one with the sewage to the sea
what did i know about waters rushing back
what did i know about drowning
or being drowned

you would have been born into winter
in the year of the disconnected gas
and no car   we would have made the thin
walk over Genesee hill into the Canada wind
to watch you slip like ice into strangers' hands
you would have fallen naked as snow into winter
if you were here i could tell you these
and some other things

if i am ever less than a mountain
for your definite brothers and sisters
let the rivers pour over my head
let the sea take me for a spiller
of seas   let black men call me stranger
always   for your never named sake

JANE DURAN
Stillborn

This hurt has beat so long,
turns up with the tide
each month – memorial.

The midwife waits by the bed.
A hand rests on my belly,
trails its design
with sympathy.
Who weeps with me?
I do not recognise
the long white hair.

Bygone a fire escape
a point of entry
a wedge.
The fire hand is austere
all night long
all labour long
undoing.

I touch your foot
before you go
stepping blindly off
no toehold, no notches
to catch at
nothing binding, nothing soft

our child
dropped down through time
through the slats
like a dime.

Here in my bed
I exchange coinage with the night.
The curtain whisks up – seagull edge,
its white barely flaring.
The roof is smitten with rain
and the ends of stories.

PETER FALLON
A Part of Ourselves

Forewarned but not forearmed –
no, not for this.
A word first whispered months ago
and longed for longer tripped on the tongue,
a stammer, now a broken promise.

Averted eyes. Uncertain talk
of a certain strange condition.
The scanned screen slips out of focus,
a lunar scene, granite shapes, shifting.
We bent beneath the weight of attrition

knowing it might have been worse.

We were visited.
Now the minutes are grief
or grief postponed – not to remember
seems to betray; laughter would be sacrilege.
We will find a way to mind him as a leaf

who fell already from the family tree,
crushed. He hadn't a chance.
We pray at best for the open wound
to grow a scar.
We welcome him his deliverance.

There are things worse than death.

Imagine a man not wanting to live
who could. Now he lies in an oxygen tent
in the whispered kindness of nurses.
Night and day are one to him,
his without hunger, just bewilderment

and quiet uncomplaining. Brightly lit.
He seems to breathe another air.
There's a photograph in *The Best of LIFE:*
A summary execution, Budapest, October 1956.
He flinched that way from the snapshot glare

of the world laid out for him.

96

So they gave her sedatives.
I sought and found the comfort of a friend.
She tendered brave communion
in the early hours
as I waited, waited, for the given end.

There are more hurts than cures.
Already we'd begun talking
the hushed courtesies of loss.
Then, at dawn, the telephone.
It seems I've been sleepwalking

since.

We broached the sorrow hoard
of women, tales unmentioned in their marriages,
unsaid to friends, to families.
Fellow feeling loosed their tongues
about unwanted pregnancies, abortions, miscarriages,

as his remains, a fingerful of hair,
a photograph, his cold kiss called, 'Remember me,'
and I stood with them at the lip
of graves. She cried from miles away,
'I miss my baby,' as an amputee

laments a phantom limb.

Time and again, for years on years,
I've thought about a corner of Loughcrew,
a three-foot plot for 'Henry Timson,
born and died September 2nd, 1899',
sheltered under ivy-overgrown yew,

and wondered how you'd walk away from burying
a child. Little I knew. Now the sound
of a cousin's prayers and Pa Grimes' spade
wheels me round and her sudden, 'We are leaving
a part of ourselves in that ground.'

The innocent part.

He'll die again at Christmas every year.
We felt the need grow all night
to give him a name, to assert him
as a member of our care, to say he was
alive. Oh, he lived all right,

he lived a lifetime. Now certain sounds,
sights and smells are the shibboleth
of a season. In a hospital corridor
I held him in my arms. I held him tight.
His mother and I, we held our breath –

and he held his.

LIZ HOUGHTON
Caustic Soda

The week the first baby died
my father visited –
awkward and lost in the new house
with stains on the floor
that would not fade.

While I was crying in hospital
he was on his knees,
not praying – scrubbing
with caustic soda and wire wool –
heedless for hours
with no gloves on.

He hid his red and bleeding hands –
said he hadn't felt the pain.
I held them gently, scolding,
not needing to say
that I'd learned how it feels
to love your child that way.

DEREK WALCOTT
from Early Pompeian

IV

As for you, little star,
my lost daughter, you are
bent in the shape forever
of a curled seed sailing the earth,
in the shape of one question, a comma
that knows before us whether death
is another birth.
            I had no answer
to that tap-tapping under the dome
of the stomach's round coffin.
I could not guess whether you were calling
to be let in, or to be let go
when the door's groaning blaze
seared the grape-skin
frailty of your eyes crying
against our light, and all that is kin
to the light.
You had sailed without any light
your seven months on the amniotic sea.
You never saw your murderer,
your birth and death giver,
but I will see you everywhere,
I will see you in a boneless
sunbeam that strokes the texture
of things – my arm, the pulseless arm
of an armchair, an iron railing, the leaves
of a dusty plant by a closed door,
in the beams of my own eyes in a mirror.
The lives that we must go on with
are also yours. So I go on
down the apartment steps to the hot
streets of July the twenty-second, nineteen
hundred and eighty, in Trinidad,
amazed that trees are still green
around the Savannah, over the Queen's
Park benches, amazed that my feet can carry
the stone of the earth, the heavier stone of the head,

and I pass through shade where a curled
blossom falls from a black, forked branch
to the asphalt, soundlessly. No cry.
You knew neither this world nor the next,
and, as for us, whose hearts must never harden
against ourselves, who sit on a park bench
like any calm man in a public garden
watching the bright traffic,
we can only wonder why a seed should envy
our suffering, to flower, to suffer,
to die. Gloria, Perdita, I christen
you in the shade, on the bench,
with no hope of the resurrection.
Pardon. Pardon the pride I have taken
in a woman's agony.

JOHN CROWE RANSOM
Dead Boy

The little cousin is dead, by foul subtraction,
A greenbough from Virginia's aged tree,
And none of the countrykin like the transaction,
Nor some of the world of outer dark, like me.

A boy not beautiful, nor good, nor clever,
A black cloud full of storms too hot for keeping,
A sword beneath his mother's heart – yet never
Woman bewept her babe as this is weeping,

A pig with a pasty face, so I had said,
Squealing for cookies, kinned by poor pretense
With a noble house. But the little man quite dead,
I see the forbears' antique lineaments.

The elder men have strode by the box of death
To the wide flag porch, and muttering low send round
The bruit of the day. O friendly waste of breath!
Their hearts are hurt with a deep dynastic wound.

He was pale and little, the foolish neighbors say;
The first-fruits, saith the Preacher, the Lord hath taken;
But this was the old tree's late branch wrenched away,
Grieving the sapless limbs, the shorn and shaken.

SEAMUS HEANEY
The Summer of Lost Rachel

Potato crops are flowering,
 Hard green plums appear
On damson trees at your back door
 And every berried briar

Is glittering and dripping
 Whenever showers plout down
On flooded hay and flooding drills.
 There's a ring around the moon.

The whole summer was waterlogged
 Yet everyone is loath
To trust the rain's soft-soaping ways
 And sentiments of growth

Because all confidence in summer's
 Unstinting largesse
Broke down last May when we laid you out
 In white, your whited face

Gashed from the accident, but still,
 So absolutely still,
And the setting sun set merciless
 And every merciful

Register inside us yearned
 To run the film back,
For you to step into the road
 Wheeling your bright-rimmed bike,

Safe and sound as usual,
    Across, then down the lane,
The twisted spokes all straightened out,
    The awful skid-marks gone.

But no. So let the downpours flood
    Our memory's riverbed
Until, in thick-webbed currents,
    The life you might have led

Wavers and tugs dreamily
    As soft-plumed waterweed
Which tempts our gaze and quietens it
    And recollects our need.

III. Friends making off
ahead of time...

WILLIAM MEREDITH
In Loving Memory of the Late Author
of the *Dream Songs*

Friends making off ahead of time
on their own, I call that willful, John,
but that's not judgment, only argument
such as we've had before.
I watch a shaky man climb
a cast-iron railing in my head, on
a Mississippi bluff, though I had meant
to dissuade him. I call out, and he doesn't hear.

'Fantastic! Fantastic! Thank thee, dear Lord,'
is what you said we were to write on your stone,
but you go down without so much as a note.
Did you wave jauntily, like the German ace
in a silent film, to a passer-by, as the paper said?
We have to understand how you got
from here to there, a hundred feet straight down.
Though you had told us and told us,
and how it would be underground
and how it would be for us left here,
who could have plotted that swift chute
from the late height of your prizes?
For all your indignation, your voice
was half howl only, half of it was caress.
Adorable was a word you threw around,
fastidious John of the gross disguises,
and there was another: 'this work of almost *despair*.'

Morale is what I think about all the time
now, what hopeful men and women can say and do.
But having to speak for you, I can't
lie. 'Let his giant faults appear, as sent
together with his virtues down,' the song says.
It says suicide is a crime
and that wives and children deserve better than this.
None of us deserved, of course, you.

FEDERICO GARCÍA LORCA
Nocturnes of the Window (4)
(translated from the Spanish by Merryn Williams)

Today, in the reservoir,
a child has died in the water.
Now she is out of the pool,
laid on the earth and shrouded.

From her head to her thighs
a fish crosses her, calls her.
The wind says, 'Child',
but they cannot wake her.

The reservoir has loosened
its hair of seaweed,
stripped to the air its grey breasts
shaken by frogs.

God save you. We'll pray
to Our Lady of Water
for the child from the reservoir,
under the apples, dead.

Soon I'll lay
two little gourds beside her
that she may float,
alas! on the salt sea.

JACK HIRSCHMAN
Asa

I can't conceive of you that way
without my skull filling with our belly laughter, and the curve
of a dirtpath down the lots at the end of a street in The Bronx.

Old friend, see what you went and did?
kicked the bucket with your tin leg
down the long final stoop, and the dead neighborhood
came alive as if for a fire.

Now I carry a head at my side, thigh-high,
in my hands held up to the sun,
on my shoulder, on my arm,
in my thought at the tip of my pen
I carry an essence of Asa
who was brother though not blood,
a palm on the shoulder of childhood,
a sway of the magic of the poem,
who went off to war
and living afterward in exile
kept a fingerpoint on me
that made the island far away next door.

For a spell of years we traveled the poem together,
though continents apart, by in and exhaling
gematrias of the art of the jazz of words –
   'Chances are...'
      Chance hasard
         Chance is czar

about covers it,
and the design therein
of all those paths where seraphs and serifs
and sephers multiplied

I'll always see him, arms widespread, skipping and jumping
at the top of the steps of the sublime stoop,
which were the forms of his poems themselves,
put together, mundane with arcane,
by his lifting of the letters by the seats of their pants,

turning them over and inside out,
making pacts with the absences within and between them,
dancing them down to the pitchpenny street
and through the cracks making books
of pinpointedly succinct sophisticated alchemies
that could mint new Abrahams at the bottom of the Yellow River
in the Third Century B.C. and make them sound
like daffodils on Hebden Heath.

It was always bright darkness when Asa at table
spelled out the lineage of alphabets and trees,

dazzling the babblers with his style of understatement,
perfectly inserted like a synchrony,

and the seams of paranoia would split at his hip
deep self-deprecations,

and the wood as if hypnotised stripped to its
mystic glyphs.

Now he's supposed to be one with the spaces between and around
and within the letters he most adored,
a style and content at last,
but the bucket's anxious racket as it tumbles
sounds like Fire!
and the ladders called out simply won't lie down
precisely because they're also your poems.

I just can't conceive of you that way
without my skull filling with our belly laughter, and the curve
of a dirtpath down the lots at the end of a street in The Bronx.

A little kid can turn on it
with a stompy clomp of dust,
in knee-pants, tee-shirt,
knickers in the fall.

You did.
Me too.

Meet you there after school.

DAVID GASCOYNE
An Elegy
(R.R. 1916-41)

Friend, whose unnatural early death
In this year's cold, chaotic Spring
Is like a clumsy wound that will not heal:
What can I say to you, now that your ears
Are stoppered-up with distant soil?
Perhaps to speak at all is false; more true
Simply to sit at times alone and dumb
And with most pure intensity of thought
And concentrated inmost feeling, reach
Towards your shadow on the years' crumbling wall.

I'll say not any word in praise or blame
Of what you ended with the mere turn of a tap;
Nor to explain, deplore nor yet exploit
The latent pathos of your living years –
Hurried, confused and unfulfilled –
That were the shiftless years of both our youths
Spent in the monstrous mountain-shadow of
Catastrophe that chilled you to the bone;
The certain imminence of which always pursued
You from your heritage of fields and sun...

I see your face in hostile sunlight, eyes
Wrinkled against its glare, behind the glass
Of a car's windscreen, while you seek to lose
Your self in swift devouring of white roads
Unwinding across Europe or America;
Taciturn at the wheel, wrapped in a blaze
Of restlessness that no fresh scene can quench;
In cities of brief sojourn that you pass
Through in your quest for respite, heavy drink
Alone enabling you to bear each hotel night.

Sex, Art and Politics: those poor
Expedients! You tried them each in turn,
With the wry inward smile of one resigned
To join in every complicated game
Adults affect to play. Yet girls you found
So prone to sentiment's corruptions; and the joy
Of sensual satisfaction seemed so brief, and left
Only new need. It proved hard to remain
Convinced of the Word's efficacity; or even quite
Certain of World-Salvation through 'the Party Line...'

Cased in the careful armour that you wore
Of wit and nonchalance, through which
Few quizzed the concealed countenance of fear,
You waited daily for the sky to fall;
At moments wholly panic-stricken by
A sense of stifling in your brittle shell:
Seeing the world's damnation week by week
Grow more and more inevitable; till
The conflagration broke out with a roar,
And from those flames you fled through whirling smoke,

To end at last in bankrupt exile in
That sordid city, scene of *Ulysses*; and there,
While War sowed all the lands with violent graves,
You finally succumbed to a black, wild
Incomprehensibility of fate that none could share...
Yet even in your obscure death I see
The secret candour of that lonely child
Who, lost in the storm-shaken castle-park,
Astride his crippled mastiff's back was born
Slowly away into the utmost dark.

HOWARD MOSS
Water Island
(to the memory of a friend, drowned off Water Island, April 1960)

Finally, from your house there is no view;
The bay's blind mirror shattered over you
And Patchogue took your body like a log
The wind rolled up to shore. The senseless drowned
Have faces nobody would care to see,
But water loves those gradual erasures
Of flesh and shoreline, greenery and glass,
And you belonged to water, it to you,
Having built, on a hillock, above the bay,
Your house, the bay giving you reason to,
Where now, if seasons still are running straight,
The horseshoe crabs clank armor night and day,
Their couplings far more ancient than the eyes
That watched them from your porch. I saw one once
Whose back was a history of how we live;
Grown onto every inch of plate, except
Where the hinges let it move, were living things,
Barnacles, mussels, water weeds – and one
Blue bit of polished glass, glued there by time:
The origins of art. It carried them
With pride, it seemed, as if endurance only
Matters in the end. Or so I thought.

Skimming traffic lights, starboard and port,
Steer through planted poles that mark the way,
And other lights, across the bay, faint stars
Lining the border of Long Island's shore,
Come on at night, they still come on at night,
Though who can see them now I do not know.
Wild roses, at your back porch, break their blood,
And bud to test surprises of sea air,
And the birds fly over, gliding down to feed
At the two feeding stations you set out with seed,
Or splash themselves in a big bowl of rain
You used to fill with water. Going across
That night, too fast, too dark, no one will know,
Maybe you heard, the last you'll ever hear,

The cry of the savage and endemic gull
Which shakes the blood and always brings to mind
The thought that death, the scavenger, is blind,
Blunders and is stupid, and the end
Comes with ironies so fine the seed
Falters in the marsh and the heron stops
Hunting in the weeds below your landing stairs,
Standing in a stillness that now is yours.

JOSEPH LANGLAND
War

When my young brother was killed
By a mute and dusty shell in the thorny brush
Crowning the boulders of the Villa Verde Trail
On the island of Luzon,

I laid my whole dry body down,
Dropping my face like a stone in a green park
On the east banks of the Rhine;

On an airstrip skirting the Seine
His sergeant brother sat like a stick in his barracks
While cracks of fading sunlight
Caged the dusty air;

In the rocky rolling hills west of the Mississippi
His father and mother sat in a simple Norwegian parlor
With a photograph smiling between them on the table
And their hands fallen into their laps
Like sticks and dust;

And still other brothers and sisters,
Linking their arms together,
Walked down the dusty road where once he ran
And into the deep green valley
To sit on the stony banks of the stream he loved
And let the murmuring waters
Wash over their blood-hot feet with a springing crown of tears.

112

EVGENY VINOKOUROV

Eyes

(translated from the Russian by Anthony Rudolf)

Exploded. To the ground. On his back. Arms apart. He
Raised himself to his knees, and bit his lips.
Across his face were smeared not tears
But eyes shot out.

Awful, awful. Bent double, I heaved
Him to one side. He was all
Covered with clay. I could hardly
Drag him across to the village.

In the field-hospital he cried
To the nurse: 'Oh it hurts! When you change
The bandage it's hell!' And I gave him, as one does,
Something to smoke as he lay dying.

And when (taking him away) the wheels began
To whimper sharply, over all the voices
I suddenly remembered, for the first time:
My friend had pale blue eyes.

LIZ HOUGHTON

My Spring Season's Ending

> *I have lost you, my brother*
>   *and your death has ended*
> *the spring season*
>   *of my happiness.*
> CATULLUS

Being younger, I wasn't allowed
the silver, steely thrill
of the slide –
the slippery shock
and blue liquid landing.

The water was too deep,
but he would be at the end,
a colossus of safety
with his seven years advantage.

I didn't look,
my faith complete,
but was dragged from the water
after two trips to the bottom.
On the silent journey home
I suffered the loss of him
as he wrestled with remorse.

Years later
on another silent journey
I remembered.
A slick of oil
had caught his bike wheel
and sent him headlong.
Grief-stripped of logic
I knew I should have caught him
or died in the attempt.

REED WHITTEMORE
On the Suicide of a Friend

Some there are who are present at such occasions,
And conduct themselves with appropriate feeling and grace.
But they are the rare ones. Mostly the friends and relations
Are caught playing cards or eating miles from the place.
What happens on that dark river, or road, or mountain
Passes unnoticed as friend trumps loved one's ace.
Perhaps he knew this about them – worse, he did not,
And raged over the brink of that road or mountain
Thinking at least they'd remember before they forgot.
Either way, now he is dead and done with that lot.

FEDERICO GARCÍA LORCA
Suicide

(Perhaps it happened because you did not know your geometry)

(translated from the Spanish by Merryn Williams)

The boy was growing faint and weak.
It was morning, ten o'clock.

His heart was filled with broken wings
and rag-flowers, feeble worthless things.

He felt that there was only one
word for his mouth to close upon.

On taking off his gloves, he saw
soft ashes falling to the floor.

Through the window, he saw a tower.
He was the window and the tower.

No doubt he also saw the clock
watch him, unmoving in its box.

He saw his quiet shadow stretched
flat out upon the white silk couch.

And, geometrical and rigid,
he broke the mirror with a hatchet.

At which, a giant jet of gloom
burst into the unreal room.

ERICA JONG
The Lure of the Open Window
(in memory of Joel Lieber)

> *Truth has very few friends and those few are suicides*
> ANTONIO PORCHIA

The mouth of the night is open.
It wants to eat me.
It says the stars are lonely for me.
It lures me
with a faint wind
like a song.

This window
is the exit of the world.
Beyond it hover
my friends who have stepped off the earth,
out of themselves.
Like beginning swimmers,
they are treading air.

Why does the window
sing to me that way?

At the bottom of the pit
are alley cats & bottle glass
not truth.

Twenty windy stories down,
would I become
wholly myself?

The window hisses.

It is trying to blow out
this poem.

VERNON SCANNELL
In Memoriam P.A.L., 2.12.85

I heard the news at one o'clock,
Formal from the radio;
The room seemed sharply cold as though
The air itself had suffered shock.

I was surprised by how those words,
So calmly voiced, could penetrate
The idling heart and resonate
Like softly falling minor thirds.

We met each other once, that's all,
Nearly twenty years ago.
We were not close and yet I know
His death-day stretched beneath a pall

Of melancholy that would leave
Something of its gloom behind,
A broken cord, half-lowered blind,
Although we may forget we grieve.

Of all that happened on that day
Of snivelling December rain
One thing chiefly chimes again:
I did not weep or curse or pray,

But petulantly cried aloud,
'I do not want him to be dead!'
He would have smiled to hear this said
If he had heard from some high cloud.

Yet I believe that smile would be,
Although ironic, kindly too,
For who would approbate the true
Voice of feeling more than he?

CLAUDE VIGÉE
A Phonecall from New York
(translated from the French by Anthony Rudolf)

All our friends have left to dance
the night away
under the rainy earth.
Soon we shall be the only ones
turning in the night
among strangers who pass by
and do not see us
and do not speak to us
in human language.

Why do the dying burn
devoured by fever
if not to freeze tomorrow
in the grey dawn
in the winter mud?
And why must they cry
throughout the night,
to die in the morning
their hair matted in sweat?

Soon we shall wander
lost
among these strangers
with whom we had never danced,
nor laughed:
they would not have even
recognised our faces
in the improbable brightness
of original dawn.

Already our playmates have left us;
one by one, without saying a word,
they have signed up for winter sports
in the school of oblivion.
Bending in the December rain
the storm decks out with brief cold stars,
a single cypress tree
sparkles as it whirls
in the squally darkness.

LOUIS MACNEICE
The Suicide

And this, ladies and gentlemen, whom I am not in fact
Conducting, was his office all those minutes ago,
This man you never heard of. There are the bills
In the intray, the ash in the ashtray, the grey memoranda stacked
Against him, the serried ranks of the box-files, the packed
Jury of his unanswered correspondence
Nodding under the paperweight in the breeze
From the window by which he left; and here is the cracked
Receiver that never got mended and here is the jotter
With his last doodle which might be his own digestive tract
Ulcer and all or might be the flowery maze
Through which he had wandered deliciously till he stumbled
Suddenly finally conscious of all he lacked
On a manhole under the hollyhocks. The pencil
Point had obviously broken, yet, when he left this room
By catdrop sleight-of-foot or simple vanishing act,
To those who knew him for all that mess in the street
This man with the shy smile has left behind
Something that was intact.

JILL BAMBER
Falling

She fell between the bed and the commode
and everything was out of reach that night
except the quilt she dragged onto the floor,
wrapped herself inside its padded roses
down there among dropped shoes and safety-pins.

That night I dreamed of a bird with a broken wing
I cradled in my arms but couldn't save
and lost its message in the blur of sleep,
while she, who'd felt my first faint quickening
held anxious fingers to her thread-like pulse.

Imprinted like a grey-lag goose she lay
until the dawn laid creeping bars of light
across the carpet's blue and zig-zag lines.
Sometime then she drifted, floating free,
with questions left, with so much still unsaid.

I meet the blank denial of the wall
where only yesterday a mirror hung
letting in the distance. Then it slipped.
No one saw until the helper came,
her early morning call raw with the news.

R.S. THOMAS
Death of a Peasant

You remember Davies? He died, you know,
With his face to the wall, as the manner is
Of the poor peasant in his stone croft
On the Welsh hills. I recall the room
Under the slates, and the smirched snow
Of the wide bed in which he lay,
Lonely as an ewe that is sick to lamb
In the hard weather of mid-March.
I remember also the trapped wind
Tearing the curtains, and the wild light's
Frequent hysteria upon the floor,
The bare floor without a rug
Or mat to soften the loud tread
Of neighbours crossing the uneasy boards
To peer at Davies with gruff words
Of meaningless comfort, before they turned
Heartless away from the stale smell
Of death in league with those dank walls.

MARTIN BELL
Letter to a Friend

Dear Russ, you're dead and dust. I didn't know.
I've heard it only at removes. For X,
Whom we detested, passed it on from Y,
For whom we had a jeering kind of fondness –
He read about it in the Old School Journal –
One way of keeping up.

'Organic disease' were the words. Which one?
Which painful monster had you when you died?
As good a life as me, I would have said –
You're one-up now, you smug old bastard:
'Christ, boy,' you say, 'I'm dead now.'
Stop dribbling bubbles of laughter round your pipe.

How many years since both of us owed letters?
Let's offer the usual excuses –
Marriage, of course, wives don't get on,
The housing-shortage, railway fares, etc.,
Weak putting-off, sheer bloody laziness.
We didn't want to say the way things went
Pissed on the hopes we entertained,
Naive, of course, but vivid, and still pissed on –
The old gang born again in young careerists –
(Christ, boy, they're reading *The Times* now!)
As if we hadn't known all this before!

Gratitude, now, is what's appropriate,
How glad I am I've had your company!
After an adolescent's silly days
Of idle mornings, hypochondriac afternoons,
Thick skies that frowned, and trees that swayed foreboding,
What evenings of relief have set me free!

Evenings of beer and talk, bezique, Tchaikovsky,
Hysterical evenings screeching at dull flicks,
And evenings when we gossiped into movement
The huge grotesques we knew, to keep us sane –
Hadji, Wokko, Nodger hardly knew themselves
And should we meet would start us off again.

'Christ, boy,' you say, 'Listen to this.'
Something new, I expect, about Taverner's sponges,
Drying, between the lying maps, in rows.
The sods today are duller and more utter,
But deadlier, deadlier still.

A formal ending I can't manage.
We've been solemn enough before, at Party meetings,
Constructive, eager, serious, ineffective...
'Yours fraternally,' then. And grin your inverted commas.
Help me to tell the truth and not feel dull.

EDWARD LUCIE-SMITH
The Lesson

'Your father's gone,' my bald headmaster said.
His shiny dome and brown tobacco jar
Splintered at once in tears. It wasn't grief.
I cried for knowledge which was bitterer
Than any grief. For there and then I knew
That grief has uses – that a father dead
Could bind the bully's fist a week or two;
And then I cried for shame, then for relief.

I was a month past ten when I learnt this;
I still remember how the noise was stilled
In school-assembly when my grief came in.
Some goldfish in a bowl quietly sculled
Around their shining prison on its shelf.
They were indifferent. All the other eyes
Were turned towards me. Somewhere in myself
Pride, like a goldfish, flashed a sudden fin.

PENNY SOWERBY
Grown-up

He died one February: before I had got dressed
you saw me, in pyjamas, watch him chilling on the couch
and said we'd strip the bed. The sheets
and blankets off, you had me muffled up
in jumpers, out the house and in the car
your jazz tapes playing on the only decent speakers
that we had: your driving ones.

We carried all the bedding from the car
and up the drive to the launderette, and pushed it in,
and watched the creases fall, and fall, and fall
and after chocolate, and thinning magazines
I helped you fold, walking towards you
with two hot corners of a rug
while back at home the undertaker
chattered up the path
bleakly.

Bank Holiday when you died: even colder.
Found me driving to the closed launderette
with a car full of blankets
wanting to bang on the door
to let me back in.

LIBBY HOUSTON
Post-War

In 1943
my father
dropped bombs on the continent

I remember
my mother
talking about bananas
in 1944

when it rained,
creeping alone to the windowsill
I stared up the hill,
watching, watching,
watching without a blink
for the Mighty Bananas
to stamp through the Blitz

they came in paper bags
in neighbours' hands
when they came
and took their time
over the coming

and still I don't know
where my father
flying home
took a wrong turning

MICHAEL RATTEE
When Grandmother Died

The wind became an anger I walked into
Trying to remember her voice
As my arms raised and lowered
Clouds the color of tin roofs formed between them
In the shape of her profile
And the sounds of animals surrounded my heart
Clawing her stories from me

Intrigued by the possibilities of her own place
She had told me her dreams
Of the visible history of the air around us
Of stairways covered with centuries of sleep
Of birds with songs of coiled light
Secrets only I believed

MURIEL RUKEYSER
from Eight Elegy. Children's Elegy

...That is what they say, who were broken off from love:
However long we were loved, it was not long enough.

We were afraid of the broad big policeman,
of lions and tigers, the dark hall and the moon.

After our father went, nothing was ever the same,
when mother did not come back, we made up a war game.

My cat was sitting in the doorway when the planes
went over, and my cat saw mother cry;
furry tears, fire fell, wall went down;
did my cat see mother die?

Mother is gone away, my cat sits here coughing.
I cough and sit. I am nobody's nothing.

However long they loved us, it was not long enough.
For we have to be strong, to know what they did, and then
our people are saved in time, our houses built again.

You will not know, you have a sister and brother;
My doll is not my child, my doll is my mother.

However strong we are, it is not strong enough.
I want to grow up. To come back to love...

EMILY DICKINSON
Parting

My life closed twice before its close –
It yet remains to see
If Immortality unveil
A third event to me

So huge, so hopeless to conceive
As these that twice befell.
Parting is all we know of heaven,
And all we need of hell.

IV. Stop all the clocks, cut off the telephone...

W.H. AUDEN
Funeral Blues

Stop all the clocks, cut off the telephone,
Prevent the dog from barking with a juicy bone,
Silence the pianos and with muffled drum
Bring out the coffin, let the mourners come.

Let aeroplanes circle moaning overhead
Scribbling on the sky the message He Is Dead,
Put crêpe bows round the white necks of the public doves,
Let the traffic policemen wear black cotton gloves.

He was my North, my South, my East and West,
My working week and my Sunday rest,
My noon, my midnight, my talk, my song;
I thought that love would last for ever: I was wrong.

The stars are not wanted now: put out every one;
Pack up the moon and dismantle the sun;
Pour away the ocean and sweep up the wood.
For nothing now can ever come to any good.

EDNA ST VINCENT MILLAY
Dirge Without Music

I am not resigned to the shutting away of loving hearts in the
          hard ground.
So it is, and so it will be, for so it has been, time out of mind:
Into the darkness they go, the wise and the lovely. Crowned
With lilies and with laurel they go; but I am not resigned.

Lovers and thinkers, into the earth with you.
Be one with the dull, the indiscriminate dust.
A fragment of what you felt, of what you knew,
A formula, a phrase remains, – but the best is lost.

128

The answers quick and keen, the honest look, the laughter,
      the love, –
They are gone. They are gone to feed the roses. Elegant and curled
Is the blossom. Fragrant is the blossom. I know. But I do not
      approve.
More precious was the light in your eyes than all the roses of
      the world.

Down, down, down into the darkness of the grave
Gently they go, the beautiful, the tender, the kind;
Quietly they go, the intelligent, the witty, the brave
I know. But I do not approve. And I am not resigned.

TESS GALLAGHER
Legend with Sea Breeze

When you died I wanted at least to ring
some bells, but there were only clocks
in my town and one emblematic clapper
mounted in a pseudo-park for veterans.
If there had been bells I would have
rung them, the way they used to sound
school bells in the country so children
in my mother's time seemed lit
from the other side with desire
as they ran in from the fields
with schoolbooks over their shoulders.
Once more a yellow infusion of bells

empties like a vat of canaries into
the heart so it is over-full and
the air stumbles above rooftops, and death
in its quicksilver-echo shakes
our marrow with a yellow, trilling
silence. I would have given you that,
though these nightshift workers,
these drinkers in childless taverns, these mothers
of daughters seduced at fourteen – what

can the language of bells say to them
they haven't known first as swallows
blunting the breastbone? No, better

to lead my black horse into that grove
of hemlock and stand awhile. Better
to follow it up Blue Mountain Road
and spend the day with sword ferns,
with the secret agitations of creaturely
forest-loneliness. Or to forage
like a heat-stunned bear
raking the brambles for berries and thinking
only winter, winter, and of crawling
in daylight into the beautiful excess of earth
to meet an equal excess of sleep.
Oh my black horse, what's

the hurry? Stop awhile. I want to carve
his initials into this living tree.
I'm not quite empty enough to believe he's gone,
and that's why the smell of the sea
refreshes these silent boughs, and why
some breath of him is added if I mar the ritual,
if I put utter blackness to use
so a tremor reaches him as hoofbeats, as
my climbing up onto his velvet shoulders
with only love, thunderous sea-starved love,
so in the little town where they lived
they won't exaggerate when they say
in their stone-colored voices

that a horse and a woman flew down
from the mountain, and their eyes looked out
the same, like the petals of black pansies
schoolchildren press into the hollow
at the base of their throats as a sign
of their secret, wordless invincibility.
Whatever you do, don't let them ring any bells.
I'm tired of schooling, of legends, of
those ancient sacrificial bodies dragged to death
by chariots. I just want to ride my black horse,
to see where he goes.

TESS GALLAGHER
Wake

Three nights you lay in our house.
Three nights in the chill of the body.
Did I want to prove how surely
I'd been left behind? In the room's great dark
I climbed up beside you onto our high bed, bed
we'd loved in and slept in, married
and unmarried.

There was a halo of cold around you
as if the body's messages carry farther
in death, my own warmth taking on the silver-white
of a voice sent unbroken across snow just to hear
itself in its clarity of calling. We were dead
a little while together then, serene
and afloat on the strange broad canopy
of the abandoned world.

MICHAEL DAUGHERTY
The Man at the Door

The man at the door
wore a black armband
and an expression
of professional sadness,

doffed his hat
delicately and proffered
a hand clammy
with sincerity,
pale as
a corpse's smile.

Rain spattered
into the porch,
imposed
exclamation marks
upon the white walls
of a dark and silent
winter afternoon.

The man at the door
swore under his breath,
coughed
softly, twice,
and smiled unexpectedly.

The clock in the hall
chimed the hour,
solemnly.
Sudden laughter
split the air,
splintered grief,

like a bullet
hitting ice.

PAMELA GILLILAN
from When You Died

1

When you died
I went through the rain
carrying my nightmare
to register the death.

A well-groomed healthy gentleman
safe within his office
said – Are you the widow?

Couldn't he have said
Were you his wife?

DOUGLAS DUNN
Arrangements

'Is this the door?' This must be it. No, no.
We come across crowds and confetti, weddings
With well-wishers, relatives, whimsical bridesmaids.
Some have happened. Others are waiting their turn.
One is taking place before the Registrar.
A young groom is unsteady in his new shoes.
His bride is nervous on the edge of the future.
I walk through them with the father of my dead wife.
I redefine the meaning of 'strangers'.
Death, too, must have looked in on our wedding.
The building stinks of municipal function.
'Go through with it. You have to. It's the law.'
So I say to a clerk, 'I have come about a death.'
'In there,' she says. 'You came in by the wrong door.'

A woman with teenaged children sits at a table.
She hands to the clerk the paper her doctor gave her.
'Does that mean "heart attack"?' she asks.
How little she knows, this widow. Or any of us.
From one look she can tell I have not come
With my uncle, on the business of my aunt.
A flake of confetti falls from her fur shoulder.
There is a bond between us, a terrible bond
In the comfortless words, 'waste', 'untimely', 'tragic',
Already gossiped in the obit. conversations.
Good wishes grieve together in the space between us.
It is as if we shall be friends for ever
On the promenades of mourning and insurance,
In whatever sanatoria there are for the spirit,
Sharing the same birthday, the same predestinations.
Fictitious clinics stand by to welcome us,
Prefab'd and windswept on the edge of town
Or bijou in the antiseptic Alps,
In my case the distilled clinic of drink,
The clinic of "sympathy" and dinners.

We enter a small office. 'What relation?' he asks.
So I tell him. Now come the details he asks for.
A tidy man, with small, hideaway handwriting,
He writes things down. He does not ask,
'Was she good?' Everyone receives this Certificate.
You do not need even to deserve it.
I want to ask why he doesn't look like a saint,
When, across his desk, through his tabulations,
His bureaucracy, his morbid particulars,
The local dead walk into genealogy.
He is no cipher of history, this one,
This recording angel in a green pullover
Administering names and dates and causes.
He has seen all the words that end in –oma.
'You give this to your undertaker.'

When we leave, this time it is by the right door,
A small door, taboo and second-rate.
It is raining. Anonymous brollies go by
In the ubiquitous urban drizzle.
Wedding parties roll up with white ribbons.
Small pools are gathering in the loving bouquets.
They must not see me. I bear a tell-tale scar.
They must not know what I am, or why I am here.
I feel myself digested in statistics of love.

Hundreds of times I must have passed this undertaker's
Sub-gothic premises with leaded windows,
By bus, on foot, by car, paying no attention.
We went past it on our first day in Hull.
Not once did I see someone leave or enter,
And here I am, closing the door behind me,
Turning the corner on a wet day in March.

ELIZABETH JENNINGS
Child Born Dead

What ceremony can we fit
You into now? If you had come
Out of a warm and noisy room
To this, there'd be an opposite
For us to know you by. We could
Imagine you in lively mood

And then look at the other side,
The mood drawn out of you, the breath
Defeated by the power of death.
But we have never seen you stride
Ambitiously the world we know.
You could not come and yet you go.

But there is nothing now to mar
Your clear refusal of our world.
Not in our memories can we mould
You or distort your character.
Then all our consolation is
That grief can be as pure as this.

ELENI FOURTOUNI
Death Watch

1

Watch the flame of the oil lamp in front of the icon
and all your nightmares will vanish.

The flame of the oil lamp
hanging on the chapel's ceiling
reflected on the silverplated bodies
of the Virgin and her son –

the icon you and my father kissed
on your wedding day
now resting on the lid of your coffin
over your heart –
my name, my sister's name
the date of our birth
marked in my father's hand on the back
and below the date of his death
in your hand

Watch the flame...

Your voice hushed in the hearth room
brings promises of dreams, sweet
as rainwater
on leaves of mulberry trees

2

Yesterday
You waited under the mulberry tree
a yellow scarf with a border of thistles
around your black braids

You waited
carrying on the crook of your arm
a willow basket brimming
with white and purple grapes
and honey-oozing figs
and your frown
could not conceal your laughter
when I rushed with my sister
to plunder the fleshy fruit.

3

The chairs hurt our backs
the chapel's stone floor
chills our bones
fatigue stiffens our limbs
sleep weighs on our eyelids

Talk on, talk on I'm listening

you whisper resisting fatigue after a day
of breadmaking, your face flushed from the blazing oven,
with half-closed eyes marvelling at the ten enormous loaves
marked with the cross you trace
holding the knife between your teeth
as you knead and shape the dough

4

Tomorrow when the watch ends we will speak to you with flowers

Your friends will come
with hyacinths
sweet basil and rosemary
they will enter the large
white room
the windows will be open
the vine arbor you've pruned each spring –
carefully guiding its climb and spread –
will also speak to you with its new
lustrous leaves
it will speak to you
of the harvest we will gather alone

Your friends will place their offerings over your body –
flowers, pomegranates
and candles made of beeswax –
they will sit around your coffin
in the center of the large
white room, and will sing
moirologhia *
They will sing of the silver-leafed
poplar tree near the well
of the lark darting
through the spray of the waterfall
of gold wheatfields

They will sing
they will mourn the earth's diminished splendor

Tomorrow I, too, will speak to you with flowers

* *moirolghia:* dirges

5

I am mute now

my eyes hold
only the shape of your coffin

the silverplated icon reflects
the flame of the oil lamp

I am blind now

I remember only your face
reflected on the flame.

JENI COUZYN
from **A Death in Winter**
(for Maureen)

3

All day I keep watch.
The corpse of my friend is cool, mysterious.
The gently rouged cheek
warms in my hand like a stone.
The smell is of shit, persistent, alien

in this caring.
The incense and lavender oil and fresh
white and green line cannot budge it.

I kiss the forehead, which does not move.
I close the right eye, first timid, then braver
but like my daughter's doll it will not stay.
There is truth in this room
and I am here by grace.

The nurse who has attended many deaths
knows what's what. She is gathering
her morphines and sheepskin heelguards
all the clutter of the dying

ticking them off on her list to take them
elsewhere, where a dying body needs them.
Only the undertaker is awaited here.

In the room below us everyone is crying
except the youngest. *Mummy is dead now*
she announces brightly, to each new comer.
I hold the living bodies in my arms
see what I am holding and
what I am not holding.

Beside the window my friend speaks within me.
We look down on the pale, unblemished body.
She is joy.
She needs no reflection.
Not the dancing particles on the pond
nor black distances between the stars.

I still my mind, turning off thoughts
like gaudy lights one by one.
I still my body and enter its dark spaces.
This body I walk will die which means
will reveal that it's dead.
It is not what I am.
This universe also my body
its clusters of galaxies and rings of Saturn
its spirals and billions of stars exploding
its light-years, its mystery
is yet a reflection.
In truth, there is no universe.
It is not what I am. I am.

4

All that was necessary is gone.
Flesh and house gone.
Gone the ten thousand things.

All that was essential
clings in your daughters
moth-life, rainbow-light.

Lily-of-the-Valley you are nowhere
but within me you are everywhere
idea of earth, idea of air.

139

WILLIAM CARLOS WILLIAMS
Tract

I will teach you my townspeople
how to perform a funeral –
for you have it over a troop
of artists –
unless one should scour the world –
you have the ground sense necessary.

See! the hearse leads.
I begin with a design for a hearse.
For Christ's sake not black –
nor white either – and not polished!
Let it be weathered – like a farm wagon –
with gilt wheels (this could be
applied fresh at small expense)
or no wheels at all:
a rough dray to drag over the ground.

Knock the glass out!
My God – glass, my townspeople!
For what purpose? Is it for the dead
to look out or for us to see
how well he is housed or to see
the flowers or the lack of them –
or what?
To keep the rain and snow from him?
He will have a heavier rain soon:
pebbles and dirt and what not.

Let there be no glass –
and no upholstery, phew!
and no little brass rollers
and small easy wheels on the bottom –
my townspeople what are you thinking of?

A rough plain hearse then
with gilt wheels and no top at all.
On this the coffin lies
by its own weight.

                    No wreaths please –
especially no hot house flowers.
Some common memento is better,
something he prized and is known by:
his old clothes – a few books perhaps –
God knows what! You realise
how we are about these things
my townspeople –
something will be found – anything
even flowers if he had come to that.
So much for the hearse.

For heaven's sake though see to the driver!
Take off the silk hat! In fact
that's no place at all for him –
up there unceremoniously
dragging our friend out to his own dignity!
Bring him down – bring him down!
Low and inconspicious! I'd not have him ride
on the wagon at all – damn him –
the undertaker's understrapper!
Let him hold the reins
and walk at the side
and inconspicuously too!

Then briefly as to yourselves:
Walk behind – as they do in France,
seventh class, or if you ride
Hell take curtains! Go with some show
of inconvenience: sit openly –
to the weather as to grief.
Or do you think you can shut grief in?
What – from us? We who have perhaps
nothing to lose? Share with us
share with us – it will be money
in your pockets.
                    Go now
I think you are ready.

ANNE STEVENSON
Minister

We're going to need the minister
to help this heavy body into the ground.

But he won't dig the hole.
Others who are stronger and weaker will have to do that.
And he won't wipe his nose and his eyes.
Others who are weaker and stronger will have to do that.
And he won't bake cakes or take care of the kids –
women's work – anyway,
what would they do at a time like this
if they didn't do that?

No, we'll get the minister to come
and take care of the words.

He doesn't have to make them up.
He doesn't have to say them well.
He doesn't have to like them
so long as they agree to obey him.

We have to have the minister
so the words will know where to go.

Imagine them circling and circling
the confusing cemetery.
Imagine them roving the earth
without anywhere to rest.

JUDI BENSON
Columbarium
(in memory of my father Captain "Rags" Parish, 1905-95)

It's the misunderstanding of ashes at the airport,
confusion over containers at the Academy,
the solemnity, the familiar uniform;

It's the gun salute sending shock waves across the water,
the bugle playing *Taps*,
the presentation of the flag,
the young cadet's voice trembling;
It's the smooth leaded box slotted in,
sun glint on engraved wings,
the miniature blue and gold curtains closing –

that is my undoing.

I unravel in the wind,
so many bits of string without a kite.

DIANA HENDRY
Funeral Dance

The spire is as perfectly centred
as the black and white priest in the doorway.
Left of centre stands a large yew.
Six staunch bearers pace the path.
On the raw oak box, the shields of flowers
are heraldic crests that mock
our claims. Outside the gates
the mourners make two half moons.

Bach could have set it as a four-part fugue
but for the two shapeless figures
in sullen grey who stumble, unsynchronised
after the coffin, breaking the dance,
draining the colour out of the grass,
making the priest seem sawdust and silk,
neutralising spire, yew tree, arch.

ROBERT GREACEN
A Summer Day

Dream of a summer day: a hearse,
Bleached tombstones, gold letters glinting.
A stone forest in a city suburb.
Beloved husband, much-loved son,
Thy will, O Lord, not ours be done.
Mother in the oak coffin; yes, at last
After much pain and long, hard years
That came to nearly eighty-eight.
Voiceless I stand, her often wayward boy,
While the minister intones grave words
I hear but don't quite grasp:
'Receive Elizabeth, Thy servant here.'
Sweetest of names, Elizabeth,
Each syllable a childhood bell.
Dismay and guilt in this neat wilderness,
I don't know where to turn my head.
Down, down, down. Wood unto earth.
Gravediggers tipped. All smoothly done.
Back now to the shining city
And the Victorians round the City Hall
Frozen for ever in their sooty marble.
Gone, gone, gone, gone. All gone.
Back from the rectangles of the quiet dead.
Back to memory and guilt. Back to dismay.
Back to the nightmare of a summer day.

DUNCAN CURRY
Shortly Before Eleven

I am loading the car with cuttings
when a hearse arrives
and an undertaker looking just like yours
goes quietly to knock.

144

As I push a rose branch into a bin liner,
it looks almost routine –
a coat of polish in October sun,
a Daimler with an open door.

MIKE HASLAM
(fune-
real)

Sure, it was a sudden shock she gave us
opting out as instantaneously as she did,
knocked unconscious in the rush of spring.
        I can see her at the broken gate –
the waste elf waiting for her in the bluebell glade,
and looking back she's seeing through my eyes
and smiles. The planet turning,
and the Earth's light raiment radiating Spheroid.

The limping messenger presents the broken wings
to Death with her credentials. Case of essences
and mental records.
The polite guide, with his ring of keys
attends her patiently, at the top of the steps.
        What holds her up on that funicular?
Hello?
        A swallow on the line.
                The hearse rolls to the steps.
The beauty of the earth assumes her in its quickness.
        Ripple of recall, the sweetness
of her girlish laughter on the telephone.

Barked at by dogs she comes out blind
with her eyes wide open.
Coffined in the planisphere of Sun,
the womb becomes her in this death-conception,
and I can enjoy the pun.
        A jolt and then the carriages move on.
The vicar with her friends and kin comes voicing
interruption: *Let us sing!*

ELIZABETH BARTLETT
Disposing of Ashes

A grey day in June, as cold as charity,
The full-leaved trees sinister in heavy green,
The undertaker wearing his winter coat.
Our cold lies inside us like a cube of ice
Unmelting in the core of our being,
Untouched by succeeding summers,
For June will always be cold now,
However bright the sun, however fragmented
The light and shade, the overblown rose,
The tall grasses seeding in a recession,
The tar bubbling on the hot roadways.
Death stamps its mark on a month
And a year. Never will Jubilee tat
Be a joke any more. Sodden bunting
Hangs in the rain, swags and crowns
Disintegrate. Only the plastic flags
Survive, flapping disconsolately on fences
And front doors. It has been a wet week,
The street parties were a wash-out,
The public junketing an offence against
Private grief. Even Ditchling Beacon
Looks menacing, and the ashes not soft
As in imagination, but like pellets
Almost. We dump them among the rabbit
Droppings, and run through the mud
And drizzle, back to nothing
Where something was before,
Leaving our royal one soaking
Into the soft downland grass
Faceless to the sky.

PAMELA GILLILAN
from **When You Died**

4

When you died
they burnt you.
They brought home to me
a vase of thin metal;
inside, a plastic bag
crammed, full of gritty pieces.
Ground bones, not silky ash.

Where shall I put this substance?
Shall I scatter it
with customary thoughts
of nature's mystical balance
among the roses?

Shall I disperse it into the winds
that blow across Cambeake Cliff
or drop it onto places where you
lived, worked, were happy?

Finally shall I perhaps keep it
which after all was you
quietly on a shelf
and when I follow
my old grit can lie
no matter where with yours
slowly sinking into the earth together.

DEREK MAHON
In Carrowdore Churchyard
(at the grave of Louis MacNeice)

Your ashes will not stir, even on this high ground,
However the wind tugs, the headstones shake –
This plot is consecrated, for your sake,
To what lies in the future tense. You lie
Past tension now, and spring is coming round
Igniting flowers on the peninsula.

Your ashes will not fly, however the rough winds burst
Through the wild brambles and the reticent trees.
All we may ask of you we have. The rest
Is not for publication, will not be heard.
Maguire, I believe, suggested a blackbird
And over your grave a phrase from Euripides.

Which suits you down to the ground, like this churchyard
With its play of shadow, its humane perspective.
Locked in the winter's fist, these hills are hard
As nails, yet soft and feminine in their turn
When fingers open and the hedges burn.
This, you implied, is how we ought to live –

The ironical, loving crush of roses against snow,
Each fragile, solving ambiguity. So
From the pneumonia of the ditch, from the ague
Of the blind poet and the bombed-out town you bring
The all clear to the empty holes of spring,
Rinsing the choked mud, keeping the colours new.

CAROLINE COLE
My Mother's Flowers

Now at the end of dahlias and chrysanthemums,
Dead flowers, death flowers, flowers you loathed
I think of your funeral flowers.
Of flying from market to Clifford Street,
Even to Gillygate and Bootham to see what there was
In buckets outside that shop – was it the cobbler's
In our day?
Next to the butcher's we never used,
Priestley's who did not kill their own beasts
Like our Archie Aspinall,
But the man on the step hanged himself.

That Wednesday in early March
The shops were full of flowers for Mother's Day.
Remember the magnolias you picked from Marygate
For Uncle Peter.
I want that simplicity.
I want you to approve.
You who snorted 'arrangements'
Who raided shrubbery, border, hedgerow
For benweed, broom, cow parsley, golden privet
To overflow the Minster jardinières.
Who picked white roses from Norma's garden,
Then wrapped my bride's bouquet in silver foil
From another twenty Silk Cut.

That day there was nothing in your garden
But a feeble spike or two of winter jasmine.
The rosemary seedling's growing but it
Will never be your brittle bush.
The day he broke it I ached for you both.
Your loss and rage, his clumsiness and sorrow.

I knew how things were.
I knew when I found the pinks I'd brought you
Stinking beside the sink a fortnight on.
The house was always full of flowers
Until those last few empty months.

Now all your jugs stand empty,
Dusty on the velvet shelves of
Aunt Annie's rosewood corner cupboard,
And I will never have your way with flowers,
Though thanks to you I have their Scottish names.

All that night,
The night your coffin rested by the choir stalls
Draped by a verger in a heavy carpet cloth,
Tall candles round you,
Your flowers stood in buckets in your kitchen.
White pinks, white tulips, cream freesias and
The palest pinky roses
And in the morning I bound them with the ribbon
I bought in Dutton's for buttons,
Slipped in a twig of your winter jasmine
Although the yellow didn't go at all.
I will never have your eye for colour.

COUNTEE CULLEN
A Brown Girl Dead

With two white roses on her breasts,
    White candles at head and feet,
Dark Madonna of the grave she rests;
    Lord Death has found her sweet.

Her mother pawned her wedding ring
    To lay her out in white;
She'd be so proud she'd dance and sing
    To see herself tonight.

LIZ HOUGHTON
Hot Winds

I did not carry flowers
to the burning of my child.
Hot winds in a far country
tumbled his ashes.

A car still crawls in my head
on a blistered Australian road
carrying his white box, covered with roses,
on the day they prevented me going.

They said I should not take flowers
to that plaque next to a gravel path
where dreams cannot grow cold
and cars are daily coming and going.

CAROLINE HILLIER
Clarence

We gave you flowers when you died,
remembered your one chrysanthemum, ceiling high,
and the reek of old dog, old man.
Already windblown, they couldn't atone,
or clothe – the tawdry wreath 'In Fondest
Remembrance, brother Jack' dressed
your grave; he had dressed you each day –
couldn't shore up your need that displayed
itself, in hat and beard, pyjamas, mad dignity,
to the half-netted eyes of the street.

PAUL HYLAND
October 12th 1972
(for Lily Tilsley, my grandmother, born 1872)

The box we bear is cold
and surprisingly light.

One I love should weigh more.

PAULA MEEHAN
Child Burial

Your coffin looked unreal,
fancy as a wedding cake.

I chose your grave clothes with care,
your favourite stripey shirt,

your blue cotton trousers.
They smelt of woodsmoke, of October,

your own smell there too.
I chose a gansy of handspun wool,

warm and fleecy for you. It is
so cold down in the dark.

No light can reach you and teach you
the paths of wild birds,

the names of the flowers,
the fishes, the creatures.

Ignorant you must remain
of the sun and its work,

my lamb, my calf, my eaglet,
my cub, my kid, my nestling,

my suckling, my colt, I would spin
time back, take you again

within my womb, your amniotic lair,
and further spin you back

through nine waxing months
to the split seeding moment

you chose to be made flesh,
word within me.

I'd cancel the love feast
the hot night of your making.

I would travel alone
to a quiet mossy place,

you would spill from me into the earth
drop by bright red drop.

ANNE STEVENSON
Hands

Made up in death as never in life,
mother's face was a mask
set in museum satin.

But her hands. In her hands,
resting not crossing on her paisley dress
(deep combs of her pores,

her windfall palms, familiar routes
on maps not entirely hers
in those stifling flowers), lay

a great man shards of lost hours
with her growing children. As when,
tossing my bike

on the greypainted backyard stairs,
I pitched myself up, through the screen door
arguing with my sister, 'Me? Marry

Never! Unless I can marry a genius.'
I was in love with Mr Wullover,
a pianist.

Mother's hands moved *staccato* on a fat ham
she was pricking with cloves.
'You'll be lucky, I'd say, to marry a kind man.'

I was aghast.
If you couldn't *be* a genius, at least
you could marry one. How else would you last?

My sister was conspiring to marry her violin teacher.
Why shouldn't I marry a piano
in Mr Wullover?

As it turned out, Mr Wullover died
ten years before my mother.
Suicide on the eve of his wedding, O, to another.

No one said much about why at home. At school
Jenny told me in her Frankenstein whisper,
'He was gay!'

Gay? And wasn't it a good loving thing
to be gay? As good as to be kind
I thought then,

and said as much to my silent mother
as she wrung out a cloth until her knuckles shone,
white bone under raw thin skin.

GEORGE MacBETH
The Son

Her body was all stones. She lay
In the stones like a glass marble. There was
    No moisture in her. There
Was only the dry spleen and the liver
    Gone hard as pumice-stone. I closed

Her eyes. I saw a sole once on
A block of green marble. It was flung straight
    From the living brine, its
Pupils were bright with a strange heat. I watched
    A cat eat it alive. When I

Touched her cheek, the light failed. When I
Moved my open hand on her lips, there was
    No life there. She smelled of
The cheap soap we had washed her in. I saw
    The black hollows below her eyes

Where desire swam. I called her name
In the dark, but no one answered. There was
    Only the sap rising.
I thought of the clotted mercury in
    The broken thermometer of

Her body. It rose again in
My head to a silver column, a sword
    Of blood in the sun. I
Held to its cross of fire in a dream of
    Climbing. I swam in the air: my

Wings were extended into the
Night. I was borne above the clouds: I flew
    At increasing speeds, to
Increasing altitudes. There was only
    The sun above me. I *was* the

Sun. The world was my mother, I
Spread my wings to protect her growth. She broke
    Into wheat and apples
Beneath my rain. I came with my fire to
    The sea, to the earth from the air,

    To the broken ground with my fresh
Seed. I lay on her cold breast, inhaling
    The scent of iris and
Daffodils. There was nothing more to be
    Settled. I thought of her dying

    Words, how butter would scarcely melt
In her mouth. I heard a wheel squeak and the
    Drip of water. I touched
The cold rail and the covering sheet. Your
    Light shone in my eyes. Forgive me.

JOHN F. DEANE
Sacrament

You, pictured for ever, before me;
I stand in black
and wear a white carnation;
you, holding an array of golden roses, maidenhair,
smile up at me, and you are beautiful;
your body washed for me
and gently scented;
you, set apart in white,
a mystery, all sacred;

we are holding hands forever, dedicated;
such the signs of a deep, abiding grace.

Another image graven on my mind:
you lie, again in white;
on your breast a silken picture of the Virgin;

they have washed your body,
closed your eyes,
you hold no flowers;
there are vein-blue traces of suffering on your skin,
your fingers locked together,
away from me.

But it is I who have loved you,
known the deepest secrets of your grace;
I take the golden ring from your finger,
I kiss the bride –

and they close the heavy doors against me
of that silent, vast, cathedral.

ALASDAIR MACLEAN
Waking the Dead

The dead man lay quietly,
beamed back by candles at his head and feet
but tired, dead tired, after travelling.
He wore his Sunday suit for us
and on his face a mild surprise
as if at last he half believed we loved him.
How we fixed him with our eyes!
But if he meant to go or stay,
to satisfy the new house or the old,
he dared not for the life of him
to either family say.
And so we sat
and gave those others glare for glare
and I sat too.
With us it was not Irish lack of care
despite the whisky going from hand to hand
and the little plates of cold ham tripping after.

This was the harder land
and not a farewell or a giving up the ghost
but a presbyterian stare and business.
I leaned over him.
The air was colder and more hollow there
as if I leaned above a well
and when I dropped my stone I saw him flinch,
or I did, as it passed through.
But what the distance was between us
never never would he tell.
How many years is it since childhood now?
Yet I remember well:
'Stay, Donald, stay!' my mother said
but I said 'Donald, go to hell!'

KIT WRIGHT
Sonnet for Dick

My friend looked very beautiful propped on his pillows.
Gently downward tended his dreaming head,
His lean face washed as by underlight of willows
And everything right as rain except he was dead.
So brave in his dying, my friend both kind and clever,
And a useful Number Six who could whack it about.
I have described the man to whomsoever
The hell I've encountered, wandering in and out
Of gaps in the traffic and Hammersmith Irish boozers,
Crying, where and why did Dick Johnson go?
And none of the carloads and none of the boozer users,
Though full up with love and with cameraderie, know
More than us all-of-his-others, assembled to grieve
Dick who, brave as he lived things, took his leave.

ALAN DUGAN
Elegy

I know but will not tell
you, Aunt Irene, why there
are soap-suds in the whiskey;
Uncle Robert had to have
a drink while shaving. May
there be no bloodshed in your house
this morning of my father's death
and no unkept appearance
in the living, since he has
to wear the rouge and lipstick
of your ceremony, mother,
for the first and last time:
father, hello and goodbye.

LIZ ALMOND
'Your Father Will Disown You'

I swim out as far as I dare,
reckless in salt water.
Ocean muffles my great scream;
the caique will keelhaul me
straight to wherever he may be.
It was the sob of bouzouki
that pushed me into the dream,
rocked me with him in his cradle
of a small boat tearing toward light.

I'm home, beside my green hearth
and he spiders between my breasts,
across my heart; it's Daddy Long Legs,
his smell of woodsmoke and shaving soap
returns like the repressed until
I don't know whether I am hearing
nightingales or violins.

The voice in my head is a last seduction
it teases, it cajoles, it caresses,
it needs reassurance, it follows me
into the intimacy of my bath
for a moment of disbelief;
I shave my legs, mummy never did.

Yes I will go with you all the way
until only a handful of ash remains.
Yes, I will look after her in her grief
No, I won't tell her you love her.
Fresh rosemary flowers mimic
The baby-blue of his shroud,
Shocked by it she refuses me a look
that might have told me my body
is real which his is not.
I'm in my cot again, rattling.

IAN McMILLAN
Grief. Auntie Mabel's Funeral. The Facts.

      (unexplained light on the horizon)
I was wearing a borrowed black tie.
Our Ron held mam's hand.
The vicar had a pony tail.

      (unexplained   on the horizon)
Our Harry's face was white.
The undertaker walked in front of the hearse.
There was a woman with a tattoo.

      (unexplained light   )
My dad cried when we sang The Old Rugged Cross.
At the House they put the TV on.
It was, by coincidence, Kim Il Sung's funeral.

    (unexplained   horizon)
An old relative went out for some air.

    (unexplained light   the horizon)

CARL BODE
Requiem

So. They and I are back from the outside.
Sitting in the cold sunlight of the parlour
We agree, with no pride,
That we never saw so many lovely flowers.
Petals still lie on the rug; the heavy scent has not died.

There is not much else for us to talk
About really – not much to say or do,
Except to get up and walk
Around in the cold, scented sunlight; so I sit
Looking down, and pull into strands a piece of flower stalk.

I think, of course, of that night last year
When I dreamt that you need not have died, so that my
Mind was filled with a dull, queer
Kind of loneliness which would not go away for
A long while; I remember it well as I sit here.

And I well remember those flowers,
Thick leaves with dust on them, coarse hairy stems
Forced by late summer showers.
The blooms were large and had a flat, metallic
Odour. They were bouquets of love, they were ours.

FRED D'AGUIAR
I Buried My Father a Complete Stranger

One close day in E5 or E6, the mute hearse
rounded the corner and filled his street.

At the parlour I looked and looked
at the boy asleep. I could have kissed him
on his brow with every hair in place or wept.

We stood by empty seats shifting our weight,
drove deliberately to a hole made for him,
buried the child and took the man away.

ANNE SEXTON
The Truth the Dead Know
*(for my mother, born March 1902, died March 1959
and my father, born February 1900, died June 1959)*

Gone, I say and walk from church,
refusing the stiff procession to the grave,
letting the dead ride alone in the hearse.
It is June. I am tired of being brave.

We drive to the Cape. I cultivate
myself where the sun gutters frorn the sky,
where the sea swings in like an iron gate
and we touch. In another country people die.

My darling, the wind falls in like stones
from the whitehearted water and when we touch
we enter touch entirely. No one's alone.
Men kill for this, or for as much.

And what of the dead? They lie without shoes
in their stone boats. They are more like stone
than the sea would be if it stopped. They refuse
to be blessed, throat, eye and knucklebone.

CAROL ANN DUFFY
Funeral

Say milky cocoa we'd say,
you had the accent for it,
drunk you sometimes would. *Milky*

cocoa Preston. We'd all
laugh. *Milky cocoa.* Drunk,
drunk. You laughed, saying it.

From all over the city
mourners swarmed, a demo against
death, into the cemetery.

You asked for nothing.
Three gravediggers, two minutes
of silence in the wind. Black

cars took us back. Serious
drinking. Awkward ghosts
getting the ale in. All afternoon

we said your name, repeated
the prayers of anecdotes,
bereaved and drunk

enough to think you might arrive,
say *milky cocoa... Milky*
cocoa, until we knew you'd gone.

STEVEN BLYTH
Story

A Book at Bedtime blares from my radio
As I drive home from your funeral. Snow
Is falling, adding rust to the coat hanger
I use as an aerial. It's a reminder
Of you: those left in your wardrobe, all bare,
Their faint jangle when I opened the door.

I've turned the volume up to help me shift
A sense of shame, to try and lose it
At the next twist in the plot. The others kissed
Your lips, brow or cheek in the chapel of rest
But I didn't, you see. Believe me,
I wanted to but I'd once heard a story
About a chap who kissed a corpse. His luck
Was rotten after that. I started to think:
The long drive home, bad weather, jack-knifed trucks,
Pile-ups. I thought it best not to risk a kiss.

I pull over to rest, wind down the window,
Open my flask. The voice on the radio
Travels across the night. A condemned church
Stands nearby, its headstones askew. The earth
Is penetrated by sound waves, I've been told.
Sometimes they go so deep they could touch bones.

ROMA THOMAS
Journey

In the car
driving home through the fog
sealed inside
I shout
dead, dead, dead
why is he dead?

I rage in my steel box.
I want to drive to where you are
but I can only drive home
shouting
dead, dead, dead.

LINDA FRANCE
Bluebell and Father Are Different Words

Bluebell and *father* are different words,
meaning different things, with different
sounds. I know this from before.
Before that May's silent hyphen punctured
both, hissing dusty echoes in mauve

air. Driving home from his grave, my mother
sat in the back; his usual place next to me
carved in the choked air. *Thunder*
means weather, black, red and silver:
the sudden colours of the crash, falling

from a dumb sky; May, unlucky, in the air.
My mother like a backstage puppet,
her eyelids jammed. On her lap, the dog
barking, barking. Then, a muted silence.
No sense or sounds for sharing spill

from shapes my mouth makes. Just thin
night noises, thin air. I've lost something
so important I can't remember what it is.
All I find is no one saying the words
Not your fault. Pebbles in my throat,

pockets of infested air, I swallow them
like pills; know them well as old enemies.
Air's not what it seems, faking its cool *empty*,
its *invisible*; dreams smothered
with bluebells, wreaths of fresh air.

ELENI FOURTOUNI
The Sharing-Out

1

After the funeral,
the chants, the lamentations,
after her face received
unflinching the first
shovelful of earth,
we returned to a perfectly
ordered house – the ritualistic
cleaning up had been performed
meticulously – the smell of myrrh,
the smoke of candles
gone. The dust shaken
from the rugs,
the floors
swept and polished,
the mirrors, the photographs (turned
against the wall during
the preparations for her homecoming)
safe now from the terrible
face of her death, turned around
facing us again.
The enormous space
in the center of the room
where her coffin had been
shrunk back to its usual dimensions –
filled once more
with the usual furniture

In a day or two
the sharing-out will start –
her house, her furniture,
her dishes, her wedding ring,
and the wedding ring
of our father, and the third one
with the three rubies set among
gold grape leaves. Everything must
be divided in two fair portions.

Her dresses will be given away
her passport,
her I.D. card
will be burned by a Town Hall
official. Her telephone
will be listed under
my name, or my sister's.
In a day or two
when she will be declared
officially nonexistent
we will begin to forget her.

2

But right now
sick unto death by her long
agony – my long waiting
and guilt – on this first night
of her death, I will search her
out, here in her house
I will wrap my body
in her robe (the smell of sweat and musk
still clinging on the sleeves
and around the collar)
I will pass her combs
through my hair
look in her mirror –

her pale face
behind my face, waiting.
My face moist,
impatient, waiting for him –
gloved and white-coated-to perform
the miracle
in the empty room
below hers, on the gleaming
steel stretcher. The disinfectant odor
of her body on his hands.

Tonight
sick unto death by my long
waiting and guilt

I will take her inside me
I will eat
and drink her in
and then I will forget her.
I will enter her room,
spread white sheets
on her brass bed
and lie with him once more. Tonight
he'll perform the miracle – here
in her house – my body
under his body, under his hands that
knew her also. His hands with the scalpel
that pierced and stabbed
and cut her dying flesh
until her pulse
escaped through his deft fingers
into the sterilised air.

3

In the photograph
taken ten years ago
you are in your garden.
It's high summer, the vines
in full foliage, the orange trees
mere saplings – they shade
the entire garden now and
their fruit succulent and sweet
just as you predicted.
The photograph is black and
white and I can't remember
the color of your dress –
a flower print, buttons down
the front. There is laughter
in your eyes but the thick brows
cast a shadow. Your teeth show
white and symmetrical through
the half open lips, (what was it you
were saying?) Your hands, webbed with
prominent veins as mine are now, clasp
the small hands of my one-year-old
daughter who struggles

to steady herself on her chubby
bowed legs on the gravel
garden path – she's grown
lovely, and people say she takes
after you and after your mother
and her legs are long
and slender, as you said they'd be.
Brushing my hair this morning
I saw her in the bathroom mirror
painting her eyelids – her face moist
impatient, behind mine.

4

I brought the photograph out
of the cellar, washed off
the dust, the smell of mildew
and put it in your room, that now contains
nothing but a double mattress.
The brass bed is gone, as is
everything you had.

In the center of this enormous
white room I remembered the shape
and color of your things – the brown
velvet sofa, the embroidered cushions,
the pictures on the walls, the vases
brimming with seasonal flowers,
the dishes in the cupboard, the pitcher
of blue glass, the matching carafe.
I remembered the way you laughed,
the way you held my daughter's hand.
Ten years after you died,
here in your house
in your garden, I remembered you again
as I remember the blood in my veins
when the kitchen knife cuts
or the sewing needle jabs my skin.

MICHAEL LONGLEY
Wreaths

The Civil Servant

He was preparing an Ulster fry for breakfast
When someone walked into the kitchen and shot him:
A bullet entered his mouth and pierced his skull,
The books he had read, the music he could play.

He lay in his dressing gown and pyjamas
While they dusted the dresser for fingerprints
And then shuffled backwards across the garden
With notebooks, cameras and measuring tapes.

They rolled him up like a red carpet and left
Only a bullet hole in the cutlery drawer:
Later his widow took a hammer and chisel
And removed the black keys from his piano.

The Greengrocer

He ran a good shop, and he died
Serving even the death-dealers
Who found him busy as usual
Behind the counter, organised
With holly wreaths for Christmas,
Fir trees on the pavement outside.

Astrologers or three wise men
Who may shortly be setting out
For a small house up the Shankill
Or the Falls, should pause on their way
To buy gifts at Jim Gibson's shop,
Dates and chestnuts and tangerines.

The Linen Workers

Christ's teeth ascended with him into heaven:
Through a cavity in one of his molars
The wind whistles: he is fastened for ever
By his exposed canines to a wintry sky.

I am blinded by the blaze of that smile
And by the memory of my father's false teeth
Brimming in their tumbler: they wore bubbles
And, outside of his body, a deadly grin.

When they massacred the ten linen workers
There fell on the road beside them spectacles,
Wallets, small change, and a set of dentures:
Blood, food particles, the bread, the wine.

Before I can bury my father once again
I must polish the spectacles, balance them
Upon his nose, fill his pockets with money
And into his dead mouth slip the set of teeth.

KATHLEEN RAINE
Highland Graveyard

Today a fine old face has gone under the soil;
For generations past women hereabouts have borne
Her same name and stamp of feature.
Her brief identity was not her own
But theirs who formed and sent her out
To wear the proud bones of her clan, and live its story,
Who now receive back into the ground
Worn features of ancestral mould.

A dry-stone wall bounds off the dislimned clay
Of many an old face forgotten and young face gone
From boundless nature, sea and sky.

A wind-withered escalonia like a song
Of ancient tenderness lives on
Some woman's living fingers set as shelter for the dead, to tell
In evergreen unwritten leaves,
In scent of leaves in western rain
That one remembered who is herself forgotten.

Many songs they knew who now are silent.
Into their memories the dead are gone
Who haunt the living in an ancient tongue
Sung by old voices to the young,
Telling of sea and isles, of boat and byre and glen;
And from their music the living are reborn
Into a remembered land,
To call ancestral memories home
And all that ancient grief and love our own.

TESS GALLAGHER
Yes

Now we are like that flat cone of sand
in the garden of the Silver Pavilion in Kyōto
designed to appear only in moonlight.

Do you want me to mourn?
Do you want me to wear black?

Or like moonlight on whitest sand
to use your dark, to gleam, to shimmer?

I gleam. I mourn.

TED HUGHES
The Stone

Has not yet been cut.
It is too heavy already
For consideration. Its edges
Are so super-real, already,
And at this distance,
They cut real cuts in the unreal
Stuff of just thinking. So I leave it.
Somewhere it is.
Soon it will come.
I shall not carry it. With horrible life
It will transport its face, with sure strength,
To sit over mine, wherever I look,
Instead of hers.
It will even have across its brow
Her name.

Somewhere it is coming to the end
Of its million million years –
Which have worn her out.
It is coming to the beginning
Of her million million million years
Which will wear out it.

Because she will never move now
Till it is worn out.
She will not move now
Till everything is worn out.

CHRISTINE EVANS
Lucy's Bones

Most of our bodies will melt
letting all they ever were leak out.
Between the fires and the fresh ruins
folds of white fat
hiss and gutter till flesh flows.
But her bones will arch in the earth
not gently flexed as if in sleep
but sound as boat-staves, seasoned
timber that takes two generations to give way.

Mole-mouthed as a lover
rot will move over her
a charge of blue seed
quivering her skin, flooding
the packed, bright silks and the slit reefs,
prying under fingernails
disentangling white stalks
for the petals to fall free
and alchemize to a stencil.

Then her long bones
will be galleries of sighing
her ribcage a cathedral.
The wings of her shoulderblades
go on promising horizons, her pelvis
still pauses at the edge of its question.
The little carpal and the tarsal bones
lie orderly, arranged like pieces
waiting to clatter into prophecy.

The egg of her skull shall brim with honey.
In each eye-cave, a chrysalis
stir towards the shrouded sun.
Ladybird and velvet mite and dung beetle
seedpearls of snails' eggs
nest in the sockets of her knuckles.
In each dry crack, a patient germ.
White roots of fern and equisetum
already weave themselves a launch pad.

174

Her bones should be lodged in topmost branches
stirred at the heart of her own green storm
but her smile will shine out
through blinded ground, through deafened wind
because she stayed hungry all her life
kept her face to the edge
constantly spending
and was charged with such brightness
waste cannot claim her.

ANNE SEXTON
Elizabeth Gone

1

You lay in the nest of your real death,
Beyond the print of my nervous fingers
Where they touched your moving head;
Your old skin puckering, your lungs' breath
Grown baby short as you looked up last
At my face swinging over the human bed,
And somewhere you cried, *let me go let me go.*

You lay in the crate of your last death,
But were not you, not finally you.
They have stuffed her cheeks, I said;
This clay hand, this mask of Elizabeth
Are not true. From within the satin
And the suede of this inhuman bed,
Something cried, *let me go let me go.*

2

They gave me your ash and bony shells,
Rattling like gourds in the cardboard urn,
Rattling like stones that their oven had blest.
I waited you in the cathedral of spells
And I waited you in the country of the living,
Still with the urn crooned to my breast,
When something cried, *let me go let me go.*

So I threw out your last bony shells
And heard me scream for the look of you,
Your apple face, the simple crèche
Of your arms, the August smells
Of your skin. Then I sorted your clothes
And the loves you had left, Elizabeth.
Elizabeth, until you were gone.

VERNON SCANNELL
Funeral Games

The slow, black bell seems still to nod, its shadow
Trembles in the gloom, a musky perfume
Faint in the ear and mingling with the sweet
Blue smokey exequies and far receding chop
Of plodding hooves as she again goes in
Through their familiar door and moves inside
The still shocked house. She visits each dazed room
Leaving till last his favourite one – his books,
So many, everywhere, as if, progenitive,
They multiplied and spilled from shelves and chairs;
The recorded Brandenburgs, the piano-lid
Still raised and on the music-rest the Liszt
Consolation Number Three, the pages cold,
And, underneath the window, on his desk
Pencils and speechless sheets of lined A4
With one apart on which a few words walk,
A poem, perhaps, a letter to the times;
It does not matter now. She hoped to touch
And be consoled by something of him here
But nothing can dissolve or penetrate
The robe of ice her heart elects to wear;
These things, his toys, important trivialities,
The best of him maybe, but only toys,
As he and she might be the artefacts
And toys of hands from which they have been dropped,
Once greatly loved and cared for, but not now,
Left in different rooms to feed on dust.

ELINOR WYLIE
Farewell, Sweet Dust

Now I have lost you, I must scatter
All of you on the air henceforth;
Not that to me it can ever matter
But it's only fair to the rest of earth.

Now especially, when it is winter
And the sun's not half so bright as he was,
Who wouldn't be glad to find a splinter
That once was you, in the frozen grass?

Snowflakes, too, will be softer feathered,
Clouds, perhaps, will be whiter plumed;
Rain, whose brilliance you caught and gathered,
Purer silver have reassumed.

Farewell, sweet dust; I was never a miser:
Once, for a minute, I made you mine:
Now you are gone, I am none the wiser
But the leaves of the willow are bright as wine.

V. Holes, spaces...

GEOFFREY HOLLOWAY
Widower

Holes, spaces – not just in the small of the back
where her cushioned belly used to press,
but conversationally: missing even
those niggles about smoking less.

Missing most what was taken for granted –
the greatest, subtlest part, behind the eyes;
chasing a foam-sly figurehead without a ship,
hoping to check...the sea.

Holes, spaces, spawning themselves, endless.
That growths in her could leave such craters elsewhere! –
brutal vacuums sucking one to them
like bottles over boils, hurtful cure.

Sleepless, wanting the earthly full of her
even if varicose, unclean;
pacing, picking her ruins over
like a starved cat casing a blitzed town.

Frantic, straddling a lost smoulder
like a newspaper trying to nerve a flame;
giving up, piling the uncaught
with wet trash of regret, shame.

Holes, spaces: dragging a black tunnel,
her white shadow walking through one still...
the space in the mind, cold air;
the hole in the heart, irreparable.

MAURA DOOLEY
Absences

Your heart, like an old milk tooth
hanging by a thread: a strength we'd test
with temper, trust, the exquisite tug of truth.

Enlarged, we knew what that meant.

And now, I want your big heart here,
to chart its absences: the yellow stream
of bitterness, the silver river of malice,
the empty shore of Lake Envy,

all the landscapes it had never known
and all the different countries it contained.

JILL BAMBER
Seeing Clear

There now and always there
she stayed indoors
and never left the house
beside the sea,
her voice, down miles of wire
my fishing line.

She slipped the hook
asleep, while I was sleeping.
I breathed alone
the oxygen we shared,
remembering how she
had breathed in pain.

She watches now
as fishes watch through water
seeing clear
among the shoals of dead
and swims with me
along the blood we share.

She stabs me from
the shadow of a fold,
the smell of her
inside the dressing-gown,
drawn threadwork
round the hankie in the pocket.

There now and always there
she stays indoors
and shelters from the rain
that wets my face,
her narrow walls
explored by roots and seeds.

ANNE BERESFORD
In Memoriam
(E. Packer)

She stripped the sheets from your bed
and lay sleepless
in the blank night
fingers grasping tightly
on her own hand.

Now the fog
freezes into the bones
and you are shrouded
out there
somewhere
perhaps smiling
as the sun
slowly breathes on the white land
to clear the air.

Now the snow
frozen on the little streams
in new found woods
forms a layer of ice in my heart
which will not melt
which will not
let you leave this place
where you are joking
and your eyes ask questions.

Now in the village
is a gap –
a quick passing –
shops lack requirements
lanes are impassable
flooded
and your voice
wordless in my ear.

Well, it is fanciful
as you must know –
black veiled women with shaking hands
sort out your small belongings;
you cannot be replaced when spring comes
like rotting doors or windows
and she will mourn you
long after summer –
sadly
without fuss
the unknown grass
a reminder of your space.

LOTTE KRAMER
Post-War (6)

In France there was some heirloom jewellery,
Smuggled and hidden in the Nazi years,
Now found again and mostly ownerless.
It crouched inside my palm as family

Survivor. I recognised the bracelet
And the ring, Victorian brooches set in
Filigree with weeping rubies. Secret
Histories escaping in a tin

From gas and ash, divorced from neck and arm,
The warmth that cradled them in Kaiser's time
Or later in the 20s decadence.
Now, in this island's twilight, life or chance

On certain days will bring these items out
To give them air, to mourn, to celebrate.

JENNIE FONTANA
Carlo
(who died in the DC10 crash outside Paris, 3 March 1974)

It was negligence –
no peep-hole
to check
that the bolt
had gone home.

Your mother bangs her head:
knocks pain into a cry.

She told me she saw you
in the thick of the following dawn
on the turn of her path.

Saw you in a grey suit
she'd never stroked straight before;
saw you brush the lemon balm;
heard you rustle the chinese lanterns
in the vase on the porch.

Standing by the back door
you lit a cigarette –
waiting.

She called out
but you'd gone –
your smoke left a milky halo
in her eyes.

The vicar came to pray.
We knelt on her carpet,
by her chair,
by her sideboard with your photo
always in the centre,
by the faded marzipan pear
in the clear plastic box
you'd bought her once.

Sometimes I dream that I go
into the old shed and find you
curled up in a corner.
You tell me that you fell
from the sky
unharmed, but dazed,
and have taken all these years
to come back to us.

I lead you confused
into the darkened room.

THEODORE ROETHKE
Elegy for Jane
(my student, thrown by a horse)

I remember the neckcurls, limp and damp as tendrils;
And her quick look, a sidelong pickerel smile;
And how, once startled into talk, the light syllables leaped for her,
And she balanced in the delight of her thought,
A wren, happy, tail into the wind,
Her song trembling the twigs and small branches.
The shade sang with her;
The leaves, their whispers turned to kissing;
And the mold sang in the bleached valleys under the rose.

Oh, when she was sad, she cast herself down into such a pure depth,
Even a father could not find her:
Scraping her cheek against straw;
Stirring the clearest water.

My sparrow, you are not here,
Waiting like a fern, making a spiny shadow.
The sides of wet stones cannot console me,
Nor the moss, wound with the last light.

If only I could nudge you from this sleep,
My maimed darling, my skittery pigeon.
Over this damp grave I speak the words of my love:
I, with no rights in this matter.
Neither father nor lover.

HUGH MacDIARMID
At My Father's Grave

The sumlicht still on me, you row'd in clood,
We look upon each ither noo like hills
Across a valley. I'm nae mair your son.
It is my mind, nae son o' yours, that looks,
And the great darkness o' your death comes up
And equals it across the way.
A livin' man upon a deid man thinks
And ony sma'er thocht's impossible.

HUGH MacDIARMID
Of John Davidson

I remember one death in my boyhood
That next to my father's, and darker, endures;
Not Queen Victoria's, but Davidson, yours,
And something in me has always stood
Since then looking down the sandslope
On your small black shape by the edge of the sea,
– A bullet-hole through a great scene's beauty,
God through the wrong end of a telescope.

MICHAEL HARTNETT
Death of an Irishwoman

Ignorant, in the sense
she ate monotonous food
and thought the world was flat,
and pagan, in the sense
she knew the things that moved
at night were neither dogs nor cats
but *púcas* and darkfaced men,
she nevertheless had fierce pride.
But sentenced in the end
to eat thin diminishing porridge
in a stone-cold kitchen
she clenched her brittle hands
around a world
she could not understand.
I loved her from the day she died.
She was a summer dance at the crossroads.
She was a card game where a nose was broken.
She was a song that nobody sings.
She was a house ransacked by soldiers.
She was a language seldom spoken.
She was child's purse, full of useless things.

PAUL MULDOON
Milkweed and Monarch

As he knelt by the grave of his mother and father
the taste of dill, or tarragon –
he could barely tell one from the other –

filled his mouth. It seemed as if he might smother.
Why should he be stricken
with grief, not for his mother and father,

but a woman slinking from the fur of a sea-otter
in Portland, Maine, or, yes, Portland, Oregon –
he could barely tell one from the other –

and why should he now savour
the tang of her, her little pickled gherkin,
as he knelt by the grave of his mother and father?

                    * *

He looked about. He remembered her palaver
on how both earth and sky would darken –
'You could barely tell one from the other' –

while the Monarch butterflies passed over
in their milkweed-hunger: 'A wing-beat, some reckon,
may trigger off the mother and father

of all storms, striking your Irish Cliffs of Moher
with the force of a hurricane.'
Then: 'Milkweed and Monarch "invented" each other.'

                    *

He looked about. Cow's-parsley in a samovar.
He'd mistaken his mother's name, 'Regan', for 'Anger':
as he knelt by the grave of his mother and father
he could barely tell one from the other.

HEATHER HAND
Twenty-one Months After Christmas

I wanted somewhere to visit,
a marble slab at the bottom
of the garden to look at.
I wanted to sit
on it – run my fingers
across the face of it, pick
out the gritty balls of earth,
the way you'd wipe the sleep
from the corners of my eyes –
the dried wings of a fly
embedded in the crease of your name.

Then I wanted to lie with you,
next to you – the way I would
climb under the flowered quilt
to get in with you. How you loved
me to get in with you – our hands
clasped, the drops of your sweat
peeling down my arm like seeds.

DANNIE ABSE
Peachstone

I do not visit his grave. He is not there.
Out of hearing, out of reach. I miss him here,
seeing hair grease at the back of a chair
near a firegrate where his spit sizzled,
or noting, in the cut-glass bowl, a peach.

For that night his wife brought him a peach,
his favourite fruit, while the sick light glowed,
and his slack, dry mouth sucked, sucked, sucked,
with dying eyes closed – perhaps for her sake –
till bright as blood the peachstone showed.

JANE DRAYCOTT
Braving the Dark
*(in memory of my brother Nigel P Draycott 1957-1988
and for the staff of London Lighthouse)*

I *Search*

Passive, your glove allows me to enter
its five black-soft tunnels:
the tips however remain uninhabited,
your fingers having been longer than mine.

The words you typed and left, expecting to return,
file out across their electronic lawn.
I caress them with the cursor, like a medium
stroking the table at a seance.

At your pain on the answerphone tape my voice
sticks, as at the gaps in a Linguaphone lesson
In tears, I sort the wafers of your clothes for friends –
straightjacketed in card you watch, and seem unmoved.

At last day buckles and, awake in bed, I find you:
the deadweight limbs we turned two-hourly
and powdered to protect your baffled skin
become my own, crook'd flat along the sheet

and from the soft lame triangle that your mouth became
you breathe our childhood out upon my pillow.
Wearing the features of our father,
your frightened face sleeps inside mine.

II *Dream*

The Vicar arrives by rowing-boat,
vampire-stalks our wet front path
and batlike settles out his cloak
for The Consolation of the Bereaved

(flashback to our mother's funeral
when we remarked how very like a piece of theatre
funerals are, as his hand webbed out
a fraction on his *Book of Common Prayer*).

His head is tortoising out to kiss me.
I am trying to explain my disinclination
to dance, when you appear suddenly from the lounge,
perfectly whole, to save me.

Outside the door the road is dry again
the vicar desubstantiated. At last
we're on our own and you can tell me
how it is that you're not really dead after all.

III *Piano-movers*

They came like ambulance-men
in mufti, thick-soled
and trained to be careful

Why then must he go in red blankets,
he had played it to know,
and the virus allowed to ride inside?

In one gentle tackle they had the legs
from under it. Winded, it blurted
strange harmonies and going down was still.

He had dreamt the last test
had come negative, though upon the keys
his Hansel-and-Gretel fingers unwove the fantastic lie.

Easing its deadweight
shoulder, they tucked the flung elbow flat
and pulled deftly on blankets and straps.

'Can't you change it?'
he'd asked of the strangers
who tended his body, but failed to reply.

192

Invisible neighbours watched its wheeled
passage, bumped prone down the front path
between unknown bearers.

IV *Mahogany*

Pressing down in twos and threes
the slack teeth of the piano's smile
I try to conjure you,
your hip knuckling against mine
for just one more shambling duet.

You do not appear: I seal
the mute mahogany. Propped
on the music-rest I read
the notes you ink-embroidered
in a song for me: Lullay, and hush.

Scattered families of notes fragment
and shimmy above their own reflections.

It's a Lovely Day Tomorrow,
you used to sing
at gilt kosher soirees. Evening
lays out along the tautened strings:

the black silk thread
along the edge of your lapel
is as clear as your face
as in the dark you stand to sing
your heart out.

CHARLES BUKOWSKI
The Twins

he hinted at times that I was a bastard and I told him to listen
to Brahms, and I told him to learn to paint and drink and not be
dominated by women and dollars
but he screamed at me, For Christ's sake remember your mother,
remember your country,
you'll kill us all!...

I move through my father's house (on which he owes $8,000 after 20
years on the same job) and look at his dead shoes
the way his feet curled the leather as if he were angry planting roses,
and he was, and I look at his dead cigarette, his last cigarette
and the last bed he slept in that night, and I feel I should remake it
but I can't, for a father is always your master even when he's gone;
I guess these things have happened time and again but I can't help
thinking
    to die on a kitchen floor at 7 o'clock in the morning
    while other people are frying eggs
    is not so rough
    unless it happens to you.

I go outside and pick an orange and peel back the bright skin;
things are still living: the grass is growing quite well,
the sun sends down its rays circled by a Russian satellite;
a dog barks senselessly somewhere, the neighbors peek behind blinds;
I am a stranger here, and have been (I suppose) somewhat the rogue,
and I have no doubt he painted me quite well (the old boy and I
fought like mountain lions) and they say he left it all to some woman
in Duarte but I don't give a damn – she can have it: he was my old
man
    and he died.

inside, I try on a light blue suit
much better than anything I have ever worn
and I flap the arms like a scarecrow in the wind
but it's no good:
I can't keep him alive
no matter how much we hated each other.

we looked exactly alike, we could have been twins
the old man and I: that's what they
said. he had his bulbs on the screen
ready for planting
while I was laying with a whore from 3rd street.

very well. grant us this moment: standing before a mirror
in my dead father's suit
waiting also
to die.

MICHAEL DAVITT
The Mirror
(in memory of my father)

(translated from the Irish by Paul Muldoon)

I

He was no longer my father
but I was still his son;
I would get to grips with that cold paradox,
the remote figure in his Sunday best
who was buried the next day.

A great day for tears, snifters of sherry,
whiskey, beef sandwiches, tea.
An old mate of his was recounting
their day excursion
to Youghal in the Thirties,
how he was his first partner
on the Cork/Skibbereen route
in the late Forties.
There was a splay of Mass cards
on the sitting-room mantelpiece
which formed a crescent round a glass vase,
his retirement present from C.I.E.

II

I didn't realise till two days later
it was the mirror took his breath away...

The monstrous old Victorian mirror
with the ornate gilt frame
we had found in the three-storey house
when we moved in from the country.
I was afraid that it would sneak
down from the wall and swallow me up
in one gulp in the middle of the night...

While he was decorating the bedroom
he had taken down the mirror
without asking for help;
soon he turned the colour of terracotta
and his heart broke that night.

III

There was nothing for it
but to set about finishing the job,
papering over the cracks,
painting the high window,
stripping the door of the crypt.
When I took hold of the mirror
I had a fright. I imagined him breathing through it.
I heard him say in a reassuring whisper:
I'll give you a hand, here.

And we lifted the mirror back in position
above the fireplace,
my father holding it steady
while I drove home
the two nails.

CAROL ANN DUFFY
Dream of a Lost Friend

You were dead, but we met, dreaming,
before you had died. Your name, twice,
then you turned, pale, unwell. *My dear,
my dear, must this be?* A public building
where I've never been, and, on the wall,
an AIDS poster. Your white lips. *Help me.*

We embraced, standing in a long corridor
which harboured a fierce pain neither of us felt yet.
The words you spoke were frenzied prayers
to Chemistry; or you laughed, a child-man's laugh,
innocent, hysterical, out of your skull. *It's only
a dream*, I heard myself saying, *only a bad dream.*

Some of our best friends nurture a virus, an idle,
charmed, purposeful enemy, and it dreams
they are dead already. In fashionable restaurants,
over the crudités, the healthy imagine a time
when all these careful moments will be dreamed
and dreamed again. *You look well. How do you feel?*

Then, as I slept, you backed away from me, crying
and offering a series of dates for lunch, waving.
I missed your funeral, I said, knowing you couldn't hear
at the end of the corridor, thumbs up, acting.
Where there's life... Awake, alive, for months I think of you
almost hopeful in a bad dream where you were long dead.

THOM GUNN
The Reassurance

About ten days or so
After we saw you dead
You came back in a dream.
I'm all right now you said.

And it *was* you, although
You were fleshed out again:
You hugged us all round then,
And gave your welcoming beam.

How like you to be kind,
Seeking to reassure.
And, yes, how like my mind
To make itself secure.

LIZ HOUGHTON
Slipping Past

For years I dreamed
he survived.
I visited his home
and found him,
inert in a wheelchair.

Then the dream changed.
He was walking –
a fleshed out ghost,
but strangely young
as I out-distanced
his final age.

He wasn't my big brother –
I'd slipped past
alone.

ANNE STEVENSON
Dreaming of the Dead
(for Anne Pennington)

I believe, but what is belief?

I receive the forbidden dead.
They appear in the mirrors of asleep
To accuse or be comforted.

All the selves of myself they keep,
From a bodiless time arrive,
Retaining in face and shape

Shifting lineaments of alive.
So whatever it is you are,
Dear Anne, bent smilingly grave

Over wine glasses filled by your fire,
Is the whole of your life you gave
To our fictions of what you were.

Not a shadow of you can save
These logs that crackle with light,
Or this smoky image I have –

Your face at the foot of a flight
Of wrought-iron circular stairs.
I am climbing alone in the night

Among stabbing, unmerciful flares,
Oh, I am what I see and know,
But no other solid thing's there

Except for the terrible glow
Of your face and its quiet belief,
Light wood ash falling like snow

On my weaker grief.

GEORGE BARKER
To My Mother

Most near, most dear, most loved and most far,
Under the window where I often found her
Sitting as huge as Asia, seismic with laughter,
Gin and chicken helpless in her Irish hand,
Irresistible as Rabelais, but most tender for
The lame dogs and hurt birds that surround her, –
She is a procession no one can follow after
But be like a little dog following a brass band.

She will not glance up at the bomber, or condescend
To drop her gin and scuttle to a cellar,
But lean on the mahogany table like a mountain
Whom only faith can move, and so I send
O all my faith and all my love to tell her
That she will move from mourning into morning.

GEORGE BARKER
In Memoriam E.S.

Ah most unreliable of all women of grace
in the breathless hurry of your leave-taking
you forgot – you forgot for ever – our last embrace.

200

OLIVE SENIOR
Searching for Grandfather

I

In Colón I searched for my
grandfather without connection.
Not even the message of his
name in the phone book.

II

Along the Line I found my
grandfather disconnected
at Culebra.
              Hacking at the Cut
he coughed his brains loose
and shook

(but it was only malaria)

You're lucky they said as they
shipped him home on the deck
of a steamer, his mind
fractured but his fortune intact:
Twenty-eight dollars and two
cents. Silver.

III

What he had learnt to do really
well in Colón was wash corpses.
At home the village was too poor
to patronise. He was the one
that died.

His sisters laid him out in a
freshly-made coffin and cried:
there was nothing left of the
Silver Roll to weigh down his
eyes.

For although his life had been
lacking in baggage, they didn't
want him to see that on this
voyage out, he still travelled
steerage.

MARVIN BELL
Little Father Poem

We must stay away from our fathers,
who have big ears. We must stay away
from our fathers, who are the snow.
We must avoid the touch of the leaves
who are our proud fathers. We must
watch out for father underfoot. Father
forgave us when we did nothing wrong,
Father made us well when we were healthy,
now Father wants to support us
when we weigh nothing. Father in his grave
gives us everything we ever wanted,
in a boat crossing who-knows-where,
mist flat over the water,
the sand smooth because soft.

PETER SANSOM
5th September 1989, Small Hours

Do you exist here, where
the cat like a dancer treads among glasses
upturned for tomorrow and then on to
the table open-leaf and clothed
against an unfamiliar wall

ready for the buffet. Are you
in the chair you occupied for under a year
but almost continually the short days
in this more practical flat? Days
you spoke your mind as never before
preferring till then to let mother
speak for the both of you, but gradually
making up for it with all those vanished
friends and enemies until it became
yammering, yap-yapping, Abide With Me.
Lucid moments came less and less
to break our hearts. They came for you.
You sat in that chair, resisted,
looked up, said clearly, 'Should you go Tony?'
When he nodded, you said 'all right'. It was
everything I'd heard and could not believe,
the curled, rocking shells
in the day room, like to like,
the others to and fro in the corridor, needing
money, the way to a bus, who could not master
the cunning handles on the doors.
I cannot believe we put people
in that place, together.
You are in a better place?
I can't believe that either.
But you are not here and will not be,
not in my lifetime at least. Now the cat
is in among the bottles, brandy, rum,
whisky, port, sherry – Mother says
they intend washing you over Jordan,
that you never learned to swim. One bottle
staggers, falls, but does not break.
The cat peers down at it, and I say,
Go on then, knock another one over, the way
when mum'd tell me off you'd say, Leave him,
you might just as well tell him to do it.

FRANCES HOROVITZ
Envoi

Sorting your clothes
    – shirts, pyjamas, socks,
my mother saw you once.
I could not ask
    'How did he seem –
in shining whiteness?
– Young, or as he died?'

I wear your sweater,
    see you faintly now:
or in the mirror
    as I touch my face
a stain of grief,
    the hidden ghost.

STEPHEN PARR
Dad

I thought you should know
I've planted

your alarm clocks,
your mug and razor

and your old Cruikshanks
cycling shoes

between the compost
and the clutter of dead

rhubarb. Somehow
it seemed the proper

thing to do,
rather than just

turning them out
to the bad jokes

of the bin men
without so much

as a thanks
for everything

J.C. HALL
A Burning

The morning she brought the package down and said
'Please burn them,' I only hope my huge surprise
Didn't appear or make her feel ashamed
That now at last (or so it seemed) her grief
Had so digested every word and phrase
That to thumb through his letters still became
A dry indulgence. Laying aside my book
I took her sacrifice without a word.
'You don't mind, do you?' – I shook my head,
Not sure whether I minded but sure at least
That what I did and how I did it then
Meant, for us both, an end. I took them down –
Two hundred perhaps, all neatly tied, the news
Of school and barrack room, of how he'd come
Third in the class one week, and later found
Canada, where he trained, a friendly place,
And how after the war they'd take a cruise –
Took them behind the greenhouse out of sight
And shook them out like leaves. I doubt she saw
Anything of the blaze, and the thin smoke
Blew low over the hedge and scudded away
Down the valley. Some wouldn't catch. I raked
And prodded them with a fierce tenderness,

Coaxing his care to rest. For still his hand
Curled in the heat and words like negatives
Briefly stood out more boldly – his memory etched
On feathery fronds one moment, then breaking up
In fragile ruin.
                                    And when at last
Nothing but ash remained, I threw on earth
Like coffin-scatter, put back the hoe, went in
The kitchen way where, sharpening a knife,
She looked up, half-dismayed. I nodded, said
'They're gone,' matter-of-fact, and sat to eat
Whatever she'd cooked to keep us both alive.

ERIC W. WHITE
Farewell to Stevie

The last time I saw you was in that stuffy church hall.
Each word you half spoke, half sang
Dropped like a pebble
Into a quiet pool of silence,
Making a submarine cairn by accretion –
Your poem, your thing.
And the concentric ripples grew wider and wider,
Overlapping each other before dying away.

After the reading you came up to me with a reproachful air.
– Eric, you were asleep!
– Stevie, I protest. I wasn't.
– I could see you at the end of the row. Your eyes were closed.
– The better to listen. I heard every word.
– Your head nodded.
– In time with your A and M chanting.
– Darling, as I looked at you, I couldn't help thinking of those oysters.
– Ah! So you've not forgotten?
– What a luncheon party! Norah in that lovely red hat;
   Cecil looking like the Poet Laureate; and you ordering
   all those oysters, which took so long to arrive!

– It was maddening, Stevie, especially as you had such
   an appetite after the investiture.
– They offered no refreshment at the Palace, not even a
   glass of sherry.
– But you got your gold medal.

I still see the quick flick of your smile. But now,
Thinking of the frightened way it went out,
I wonder if you were really smiling at all.
They say that shortly afterwards,
As you lay speechless on your sick-bed,
You asked by signs for pencil and book, and firmly ringed
A word in one of your poems,
A ripple arrested –
'Death'.

PATRICIA BISHOP
Letter to Crispin

I dig in loss with each turn of the spade
let it moisten the fresh seeds.

Rough winds have done for the daffodils,
they are straddled along the beds
mud whipped
but the old shrubs survive
gold flowers and white bloom
as the days lengthen.

I am too old for spring.

There have been springs –
the centuries' ceremony
of death and resurrection
but you stayed buried.

Once I thought you would come
through those wide glass doors
carrying daffodils.

They flourished that January.

You were young
I thought you would dissolve death
come through the glass doors
and I would give you breath.

There were other springs
your mouth rimmed with chocolate.
a fist of energy.

Then snap! Running, shouting,
'You lost me! You lost me!'

SALVATORE QUASIMODO
Letter to My Mother
(translated by Jack Bevan)

'Mater dulcissima, now the mists are descending,
the Naviglio thrusts disorderly on the locks,
the trees swell with water, burn with snow;
I am not unhappy in the north: I am not
at peace with myself, but seek
pardon from no one, and many owe me tears.
I know you are ailing, live
like all mothers of poets, poor
and just in the measure of their love
for distant sons. Today it is I
who write to you'…At last, you will say, a line
from the boy who ran away at night
in a skimpy coat with a few lines
of poetry in his pocket. Poor thing, so ready-hearted.
One day, somewhere, they will kill him –

'Yes, I remember that grey stopping place
for slow trains loaded with almonds, oranges,
at the mouth of the Imera, the river full of magpies,
salt and eucalyptus. But now I want to thank you
truly for the wry smile you set
on my lips, a smile as mild as your own:
it has saved me pain and grief.
And if now I shed a tear for you
and all who wait like you and do not know
what they wait for, it does not matter.
O gentle death,
do not touch the clock in the kitchen that ticks on the wall;
all my childhood was passed away on the enamel
of its dial, on those painted flowers:
do not touch the hands, the heart of the old.
Does anyone answer? O death of pity,
death of shame. Goodbye, dear one, farewell my
dulcissima mater.'

STEPHEN PARR
Ghost

So much of you
still tethered here:
your wholewheat
loaf, its green-grey

stars of mould just
flickering on;
a feathered
shopping-list,

your old shoes unlaced
by the back door
after your last walk.
I know now

what I most feared:
to stand alone,
the precious gift I must
not turn from.

I take the path of black
roots through the witches'
circle, follow it past
lanterns of beech

and lichen
til it turns east,
climbs, releases me
into new weather.

PASCALE PETIT
Letters from My French Grandmother

Your letters are skies folded inside envelopes.

I reread the blue and cream pages
as if they are atmospheres I could breathe
absorbing secrets of the upper air.

Every Easter you enclosed pressed flowers.
A few seeds float out of the ether
and now settle on my bed.

Some words are rare as condors.
They scan the landscape of my duvet
for a safe peak to nest.

When I reach the last letter,
its untidy loops are the branches
of windswept trees.

Then there's the card your friend sent,
over which you've scrawled *je t'aime*
and kisses like black stars in a white sky.

CLARE CROSSMAN
Sequences in Jazz
(for my father)

His journal might have read:

'These copperbeeches
I hold them in my mind.
I would like to
plant orchards where apple trees can grow.'

All his life in business.
Driving every morning to the office
for meetings in stuffy rooms.
Later I would see him,
standing in the garden,
trying to make sense.
As if there were a warmth,
he wanted to claim back,
that he never wished to name.

Much later he'd turn up
briefcase tightly shut.
Sitting nervously in my cluttered room,
amongst beads and candles,
we would make the polite conversation
of passing through.

He left some flower paintings,
each detail carefully inked.
An old medal from the regiment.
And scratched records:
The Duke and Jelly Roll,
Bringing brash streets
Into an evening room.

Each tune holding
an understanding that
Like a pause in music,
or sequences in jazz,
Absence can be
The quiet distance for reflection
Before the next phrase.

DOUGLAS DUNN
Dining

No more in supermarkets will her good taste choose
    Her favourite cheese and lovely things to eat,
Or, hands in murmuring tubs, sigh as her fingers muse
    Over the mundane butter, mundane meat.
Nor round the market stalls of France will Lesley stroll
    Appraising aubergines, *langoustes, patisseries*
And artichokes, or hear the poultry vendors call,
    Watch merchants slicing spokes in wheels of Brie.
My lady loved to cook and dine, but never more
    Across starched linen and the saucy pork
Can we look forward to *Confit de Périgord*.
    How well my lady used her knife and fork!
Happy together – ah, my lady loved to sport
    And love. She loved the good; she loved to laugh
And loved so many things, infallible in art
    That pleased her, water, oil or lithograph,
With her own talent to compose the world in light.
    And it is hard for me to cook my meals
From recipes she used, without that old delight
    Returning, masked in sadness, until it feels
As if I have become a woman hidden in me –
    Familiar with each kitchen-spotted page,
Each stain, each note in her neat hand a sight to spin me
    Into this grief, this kitchen pilgrimage.
O my young wife, how sad I was, yet pleased, to see
    And help you eat the soup that Jenny made
On your last night, who all that day had called for tea,
    And only that, or slept your unafraid,
Serene, courageous sleeps, then woke, and asked for tea –
    'Nothing to eat. Tea. Please' – lucid and polite.
Eunice, Daphne, Cresten, Sandra, how you helped me,
    To feed my girl and keep her kitchen bright.

DOUGLAS DUNN
Empty Wardrobes

I sat in a dress shop, trying to look
As dapper as a young ambassador
Or someone who'd impressed me in a book,
A literary rake or movie star.

Clothes are a way of exercising love.
False? A little. And did she like it? Yes.
Days, days, romantic as Rachmaninov,
A ploy of style, and now not comfortless.

She walked out from the changing-room in brown,
A pretty smock with its embroidered fruit;
Dress after dress, a lady-like red gown
In which she flounced, a smart career-girl's suit.

The dress she chose was green. She found it in
Our clothes-filled cabin trunk. The pot-pourri,
In muslin bags, was full of where and when.
I turn that scent like a memorial key.

But there's that day in Paris, that I regret,
When I said No, franc-less and husbandly.
She browsed through hangers in the Lafayette,
And that comes back tonight, to trouble me.

Now there is grief the couturier, and grief
The needlewoman mourning with her hands,
And grief the scattered finery of life,
The clothes she gave as keepsakes to her friends.

LINDA FRANCE
Mother's Ruin

After that wedding, I breathed the sour smell
of gin, you cradling the cold white bowl, light
ghosting frosted glass; Dad laughing as you groaned
over and over *I want to die, just want to die.*

Last month I heard you, from your bedroom, urge
yourself *Try! Try!* And then I found you,
dressed, waiting on the sofa, gasping louder
and louder, your eyes wild, your lips turning blue.

What can I do but douse these images
in stiff gins, relish the mad crack of ice,
lemon eyes, soothing savour of juniper?
No one to hear me crying *Why, why? Why?*

MICHAEL LASKEY
Life After Death

After he died he went on speaking
on the ansaphone: he'd apologise
for being out and ask us to leave
our names and messages after the tone.

At first we couldn't, we just hung up,
but steeled ourselves; it was her grief,
her tape that she was perfectly free
not to choose to erase in those early days.

At last though the voice did change to hers
and we were consoled, we found we could breathe
our nonsense into her solemn machine
once more and pictured her smiling, unwinding.

214

Later we raised it – macabre was the word
we used – and she laughed, told us the truth
was tougher, more matter of fact than that:
just not knowing how to record herself.

THEODORE ROETHKE
On the Road to Woodlawn

I miss the polished brass, the powerful black horses,
The drivers creaking the seats of the baroque hearses,
The high-piled floral offerings with sentimental verses,
The carriage reeking with varnish and stale perfume.

I miss the pallbearers momentously taking their places,
The undertaker's obsequious grimaces,
The craned necks, the mourners' anonymous faces,
– And the eyes, still vivid, looking up from a sunken room.

PETER ABBS
The Singing Head

Harsh. And remote. A square for graves.
A mile from Sheringham. The coast road.
Wind warps the hawthorn. Dwarfs the pines.
Brine abruptly burns the memorial rose.
Mother mourns here, planting against the odds.
Over the inscribed slabs gulls rise and scream.
Singed petals scatter across the epitaphs.
The incoming sea's chopped white and green.

Orpheus' head churns in its own blood,
Shudders with each and every turbulence;
Battered, blind, it turns; bobs on the flood:
A severed head that will not sink,
But through the silence and the blood-stained rings
It sings – it sings – it sings – it sings – it sings.

ALAN BOLD
Widow

I see a widow standing
Stark in the winter street.
The wind has whipped
Her hair across her chin.
    She is like a bearded lady
In a sideshow.
Yet the black hat, the back
Diamond on the coatsleeve
Are also out of place:
Only
Objects of admiration
Praised by the eyes
Of those who saunter by.
    She should be dressed in white
Like a bride.
She should carry flowers:
Red, yellow. purple.
    Yet
She stands broken like
A snapped twig
Black against the winter sky
And the icy streets.
    A black streetcat nuzzles
Against her best shoes
And she reacts.
    Her life has become hollow
The way a ship does

When it sinks below
The ocean
And cadavers rise to the surface
Like bloated balloons.
Her shoes are weighted
Like diving boots
As she turns from the cat
And walks back through a sea
Of sympathetic faces
She
Will never see again.

ANDREW DARBY
Draining Our Glasses

there was a curling of fingers unlike any other I had ever seen
as she held her glass and cried so powerfully
her soft white throat tightened
and reddened like a house
builder carrying a hod

she had no idea I was watching
her every action her cigarette
smoking continually
and breathing her smoke so deep and exhaling

watching every inch
of grey smoke leave her lungs
an image
of precision and tears
her tongue sobbing out
all her memories punishing
herself for not being able to tell him
for not knowing she had loved him
and I offered her nothing more than my shoulder
as we sat in this unfamiliar pub

JANET FISHER
'There are only so many words'

There are only so many words
and I'm stuck with the ones I've got:
lines drawn desperately between roads,
the singing trees, their lost leaves,
rats running from the blaze.

'Dad died yesterday, last week, last year.'
The echoes grow fainter,
footsteps down a corridor,
swing doors and the smell of dinners,
a notice by a phone: if you are lost, ring here.

VI. It takes time, and there are setbacks...

LAURIS EDMOND
A Difficult Adjustment

It takes time, and there are setbacks;
on Monday, now, you were all ennui
and malice; but this morning I am
pleased with my handiwork: your
stick figure moves, your two eyes
are large and dark enough, your
expression is conveniently mild.
You have begun to disagree with me,
but weakly, so that I can easily prove
you wrong. In fact you are entirely
satisfactory.
              I suppose, really, you are
dead. But someone silently lies down
with me at night and shows a soothing
tenderness. I have killed the pain
of bone and flesh; I suffer no laughter
now, nor hear the sound of troubled
voices speaking in the dark.

ELIZABETH JENNINGS
from Grief

Pull down the tokens. Close your eyes,
Hide from the sun. At least the night
Will keep the pain from other people's sight
And you'll have the stars' cold light.

220

ELIZABETH JENNINGS
from **Words About Grief**

Time does not heal,
It makes a half-stitched scar
That can be broken and you feel
Grief as total as in its first hour.

ANNE KIND
Society's Demands

When the first pain is unleashed
It is acceptable to show it.

At first unbelief
Then comes name calling and
Hearing a key turning.

After seven years
It's best not to mention it
It's the way forward, they say.

It's a fine line of decorum.

Then it was: 'Time heals',
'Life must go on', 'Don't cry'.
'Pull yourself together.'

Like a sack of ashes?

The calling has stopped.
The key no longer tries the lock.
Society's demands have been met.

AGNETA FALK
I Know

you are gone now.
I know,
it's written in black and white
a paper stuffed in a drawer
for proof.
I know
I can see it on their faces as they
file past
some even running
they look so frightened
as I draw close,
that's why I know.

Yes, but you are
everywhere in the house
I know.
I feel you passing me
on the stairs
a gentle breeze.
You make up the plaster
of the walls, the entire
fabric of the house.
Your scent permeates the
carpets, curtains, every
scrap of fabric.

But, ah, you are elusive
we play hide and seek
You win   I lose.

OLE SARVIG
My Sorrow
(translated from the Danish by Ole Sarvig & Alexander Taylor)

The strange old villa of my sorrow
with cold verandahs to the north
and useless tower-rooms.

Always in the shadow
of the dark green garden of pines,
overgrown, forgotten,
shunned by everyone.

There often I walk alone
in echoing rooms of the damp
in the mouldy silence
broken only by the insect people's
scraping on the walls,

– these small crunching creatures
who in a hundred years
will have lived the house to ashes.

DANIELLE HOPE
Red Grief

In April I carried my grief with me
a sore, or a freak gene,
I knew it like my own face.

In May it would break out
when I least expected:
a knock against a window

a razor wind
a stumble on rickety pavement
a soft word.

At the end of the July
it was pleased with me.
I had changed the dressing

many times and it looked
as if it would begin to heal
tomorrow.

But in October
sometime between four and six am
the wound broke open

and I woke in shock
to the tiny heels of nightmares
capering over my skin.

LIZ HOUGHTON
The Next Christmas

My brother is six months dead
and we will fail
to make the impossible happen
round our sacrificial tree
as you pour pathetic doubles
and his daughters run to our door,
wrapped against the storm
and jumping puddles –
hampered by oversize dolls.
Beneath their waterproofs
they've been stitched
into a team: decked out
in matching dresses.

Awash with sherry the trifle
will never set.
The turkey prepares to rot –
too big for our fridge.

His wife grimly fills
her daughters' stockings to bursting.
We even take photos,
which will show our eyes glazed
like the eyes of the dolls –
sent by his workmates.
As each extravagant gift
is unwrapped I feel the tremor
of my father's sobs.

PAUL HYLAND
In Chittlehampton Churchyard

Nine months have gone since we threw handfuls of
clay-loam and shale on to the coffin lid;
the earth has settled in my father's grave.
Reuben and I have come with spades to bed

the headstone in: unweathered warm Thornback,
one cut and lettered face, delivered from
Treleven's quarry on the cliffs of Purbeck.
Reuben thinks he must dig, but I am firm;

no appetite for tears, only for toil,
for planting Dorset stone in Devon soil.

MARION LOMAX
July

Watching a different sea
to the one on which you died,
I try locking a curious gull
eye to eye.

I am with him on the roof's edge,
thinking only 'high water'.
Then, 'This time last year
I had a mother.'

It's as if one grief breeds others.
When we reached the cliff path
they'd just found the body.

After you died I felt nowhere was safe
but this familiar place
could have been the exception.

Last night I dreamt you met
the murdered girl, were
trying to comfort her.

It's reassuring to think
you'll go on doing
what you were good at –

but here we are road-blocked,
our walks policed or televised,
the streets subdued, until
our late-night neighbour
starts his 4 a.m. toccata –

and when I sleep again
you have your arm around her,
and you're saying, 'I know,
I had a daughter...'

ANN THORP
Belief

I have to believe
That you still exist
Somewhere,
That you still watch me
Sometimes,
That you still love me
Somehow.

I have to believe
That life has meaning
Somehow,
That I am useful here
Sometimes,
That I make small differences
Somewhere.

I have to believe
That I need to stay here
For some time,
That all this teaches me
Something,
So that I can meet you again
Somewhere.

AGNETA FALK
Postponing

This morning I didn't greet you.
I planned it that way and
tip-toed quietly into the day.

Come back, I tell your photograph,
sipping coffee, my eyes fixed on the road workers
laying tar. I envy their ability to move, to go on
while I sit, chained to a chair.

You stand in the doorway,
wanting to come in. I tell you to come
back later, while I'm examining the weave
on the tablecloth, preparing myself
for your visit.

You appear again without warning,
your hand on my shoulder,
tapping, tapping, tapping.

JAMES McAULEY
Pietà

A year ago you came
Early into the light.
You lived a day and night,
Then died; no one to blame.

Once only, with one hand,
Your mother in farewell
Touched you. I cannot tell,
I cannot understand

A thing so dark and deep,
So physical a loss:
One touch, and that was all

She had of you to keep.
Clean wounds, but terrible,
Are those made with the Cross.

OLIVE SENIOR
Epitaph

Last year the child died
we didn't mourn long
and cedar's plentiful

but that was the one
whose navel-string we buried
beneath the tree of life

lord, old superstitions
are such lies.

MANDLENKOSI LANGA
Mother's Ode to a Stillborn Child

You languished patiently
for months on end
in dungeon darkness
in intestinal convolutions
and indefinable chaos

You had neither shadow
nor silhouette
You had every right
to riot and complain
or raise your voice
in protest or defiance

I could feel your lust
to join the dead
living world
Your muted attempts
to burst like a Christmas chicken
into life

It is not my fault
that you did not live
to be a brother sister
or lover of some black child
that you did not experience pain
pleasure voluptuousness and salt
in the wound
that your head did not stop
a police truncheon
that you are not a permanent resident
of a prison island.

SEÁN DUNNE
Anniversary

One year dead tonight and still no sign
Of a comeback, no new recital of the lost
Lore and recipes you took when you died.
The last Mills & Boon books I gave you rest
In drawers lined with newspapers,
Racing results and pictures of presidents
Toppled long since in televised coups.
With them you are a speck in history too.

One year dead tonight and no one tells
Of the doctor falling for the swooning nurse,
His stethescope twitching near her heart.
For years you read nothing else, except
The Sacred Heart Messenger and *Ireland's Own*.
Your only cosmetic was Eau de Cologne.
You sprayed it at the air like insecticide
To hide smells: polishing made you tired.

One year dead tonight and I think
Of your aprons, the bread you baked,
Hairnets and coats, your Sunday missal.

In a city hospital before you died, you turned
From offered water and asked for the pure
Drop from a well you'd known since a girl.
'I'm finished,' you whispered near the end.
You were even too tired for love stories then.

SIDNEY KEYES
Elegy
(in memoriam S.K.K.)

April again and it is a year again
Since you walked out and slammed the door
Leaving us tangled in your words. Your brain
Lives in the bank-book, and your eyes look up
Laughing from the carpet on the floor:
And we still drink from your silver cup.

It is a year again since they poured
the dumb ground into your mouth:
And yet we know, by some recurring word
Or look caught unawares, that you still drive
Our thoughts like the smart cobs of your youth –
When you and the world were alive.

A year again, and we have fallen on bad times
Since they gave you to the worms.
I am ashamed to take delight in these rhymes
Without grief; but you need no tears.
We shall never forget nor escape you, nor make terms
With your enemies, the swift-devouring years.

WENDY FRENCH
Empty Place

A year has gone since your funeral.
It was a beautiful day,
you would have hated to be inside
away from a sun.

The pews were rainbowed by glass,
all your friends were there.
The music and poems were for you.
You should have come, I saved a place.

One wreath adorned the coffin lid,
you would have liked that,
no waste of cut flowers.
Love of the countryside was there.

I didn't wear my lace suit
you said I kept for funerals.
I thought I'd surprise you
in my old black skirt. I kept a place.

You would have imagined the birds,
the stark fields of Kent.
The music spoke wistfully.
There was much you would have heard.

We left grieving without tears,
the coffin still on its base.
It would have been hateful to see it go down.
I wish you'd come, I saved a place.

ELAINE FEINSTEIN
A Year Gone

Who believes
he is dead?
in the ground
that lies over his head
in the rain, under leaves, in the earth
who believes he is
there?

In the tick
of our blood
in the blue
muscles under our tongue
in our skulls
where a hidden ice-pick may be waiting
we must
learn

how at last
motionless
we shall fall without
breath into place

and the pain of our questions will melt like the
wax of our flesh
into silence.

DENNIS O'DRISCOLL
Siblings

I am writing at exactly the moment
you had sent me the message of his death
precisely this time last year.

Returning home from school to an empty house,
you learn the vulnerability of those
who know how thin the barrier of flesh is,

that looking forward becomes looking back
until there is nothing either way but death.
It is quiet in the office as I write,

hiding this paper under a file,
heat rising from radiators, first cigarettes being lit,
someone whistling, someone listing soccer scores.

We have spent a year without him now,
his thoughts scattered, his burden of organs eased.
This is just another working day here

of queries, letters, tea-breaks, forms.
Any minute now some telephone will ring
but I do not dread its news, as then.

I concentrate upon this moment, cup it in my hands,
to understand what the shedding of his skin
might signify and what you have lost

in these past years when home has become orphanage
and we have soiled the carpet in the hall
with the clay of their two burials,

our world refracted by a lens of tears.

PAMELA GILLILAN
Two Years

When you died
all the doors banged shut.

After two years, inch by inch,
they creep open.
Now I can relish
small encounters,
encourage
small flares of desire;
begin to believe as you did
things come right.
I tell myself that you
escaped the slow declension to old age
leaving me to indulge
this wintry flowering.

But I know
it's not like that at all.

PAMELA GILLILAN
Four Years

The smell of him went soon
from all his shirts.
I sent them for jumble,
and the sweaters and suits.
The shoes
held more of him; he was printed
into his shoes. I did not burn
or throw or give them away.
Time has denatured them now.

Nothing left.
There will never be
a hair of his in a comb.
But I want to believe
that in the shifting housedust
minute presences still drift:
an eyelash,
a hard crescent cut from a fingernail,
that sometimes
between the folds of a curtain
or the covers of a book
I touch
a flake of his skin.

TONY HARRISON
Long Distance

I

Your bed's got two wrong sides. Your life's all grouse.
I let your phone-call take its dismal course:

Ah can't stand it no more, this empty house!

Carrot's choke us wi'out your mam's white sauce!

Them sweets you brought me, you can have 'em back.
Ah'm diabetic now. Got all the facts.
(The diabetes comes hard on the track
of two coronaries and cataracts.)

Ah've allus liked things sweet! But now ah push
food down mi throat! Ah'd sooner do wi'out.
And t'only reason now for beer 's to flush
(so t'dietician said) mi kidneys out.

When I come round, they'll be laid out, the sweets,
Lifesavers, my father's New World treats,
still in the big brown bag, and only bought
rushing through JFK as a last thought.

II

Though my mother was already two years dead
Dad kept her slippers warming by the gas,
put hot water bottles her side of the bed
and still went to renew her transport pass.

You couldn't just drop in. You had to phone.
He'd put you off an hour to give him time
to clear away her things and look alone
as though his still raw love were such a crime.

He couldn't risk my blight of disbelief
though sure that very soon he'd hear her key
scrape in the rusted lock and end his grief.
He *knew* she'd just popped out to get the tea.

I believe life ends with death, and that is all.
You haven't both gone shopping; just the same,
in my new black leather phone book there's your name
and the disconnected number I still call.

ADRIAN HENRI
For Joyce Henri, New Year 1988

In 1987
Willy was 40, Roger was 50, I was 55 and you
were 52. We drank fizzy wine at your bedside
knowing you wouldn't see 53.
In 1987
sailors died
killed by missiles fired by people not their enemies
sold them by their fellow-countrymen;
blood mocked the colour of poppies
once more in the November mist,
and I
made my usual autumn note in my notebook
about willowherb.
In 1987
I saw
our remembered tree-filled square
in Preston. The school I worked in
now a wine-bar. A shopping-arcade
across the backstreets where we kissed.
I saw
walnuts fall from a walnut-tree
silently through the memory;
stocks and shares fall
like horse-chestnuts:
no laughing children
rushed to pick them from the floor
of the Stock Exchange. Only pigeons, they said,
could leave a deposit on a Porsche.

On July afternoons
we watched Australian soaps, quiz-programmes,
you propped up in your nightdress.
I brought you old-fashioned sweets,
Treacle Toffees, Jap Desserts, Pontefract Cakes.
In 1987
people took a ferry
across the darkest river
or an escalator
to the underworld
and didn't return.
The clatter of a Kalashnikov
tore through the postcard of an English village.
In Beirut
dying was Business As Usual.
She wore winceyette pyjamas like a child,
laughed with me in Liverpool, Edinburgh, Strasbourg,
Paris, and cried for you in London, though
she didn't know you. Strands of dark hair
in every kiss. Late leaves
in the Cathedral square.

And you died
not in bleak midwinter
but a rainy August.
The sun shone on Smithdown Cemetery –
when we buried you. Sue and I
worried about who would want what,
the scrap-screen, the books, the rocking-chair.
In 1987
a small boy cried at my side
when twin brothers died
in the theatre. In the real world outside
I didn't cry for you.

Will it be too late
in 1988?

A. ALVAREZ
Mourning and Melancholia

His face was blue, on his fingers
Flecks of green. 'This my father,'
I thought. Stiff and unwieldy
He stared out of my sleep. The parlourmaid
Smiled from the bed with his corpse,
Her chapped lips thin and welcoming.
In the next room her albino child
Kept shouting, shouting. I had to put him down
Like a blind puppy. 'Death from strangulation
By persons known.' I keep the clipping
In my breast-pocket where it burns and burns,
Stuck to my skin like phosphorus.

I wake up struggling, silent; undersea
Light and a single thrush
Is tuning up. You sleep, the baby sleeps,
The town is dead. Foxes are out on the Heath;
They sniff the air like knives.
A hawk turns slowly over Highgate, waiting.
This is the hidden life of London. Wild.

Three years back my father's corpse was burnt,
His ashes scattered. Now I breathe him in
With the grey morning air, in and out.
In out. My heart bumps steadily
Without pleasure. The air is thick with ash.
In out. I am cold and powerless. His face
Still pushes sadly into mine. He's disappointed.
I've let him down, he says. Now I'm cold like him.
Cold and untameable. Will have to be put down.

ANNE KIND
After Six Years

There was no sudden gust of wind
Slamming the door shut;
It closed imperceptibly slowly
On my mourning, my grieving.
Now, when death brushes past me
Towards another
Reminding me of your presence
The curtains move towards each other
The windows shake like my shoulders.

ANN SANSOM
Confinement

That winter the stairs were always unlit.
Home late from work, I'd feel my way,
unlock the door by touch
and before I pressed the switch look up, wait
to see my lamp put out a saucer to the dark.

The skylight was almost clear then,
night came down to it at once,
a movement quick and weighty as water.

At first I'd count you by the moon, by my own fingers,
half believing I could feel you in my skin.
Then it snowed for weeks, accumulating on the glass,
filtering a tracing paper air. A diffuse frost
charged the constant underwater I crossed and crossed
mindless as a swimmer, keeping time for you.

At night, in the cold sheets, unable to sleep
I began to count you in days and hours,
I named you, held your head, your feet,
felt you turn in my own body heat.

Tonight, you've slept for twenty years.
I leave an overheated house, go out
into the cold backyard for air.
A neighbour calls me to the fence to watch.
He's opening the ice on his pond. The fish come up
preserved by their cold blood, their trust.

I close a frozen room on you, your placid drowning face.
and listen to my neighbour, who has learned to wait,
obedient to the rules that govern living things.
We share a cigarette and then discuss
the nature of confinement and release.

PETER PORTER
from Ghosts

A large woman in a kimono, her flesh
Already sweating in the poulticing heat
Of afternoon – just from her bath, she stands,
Propping her foot on a chair of faded pink,
Preparing to cut her corns. The sun
Simmers through the pimply glass – as if
Inside a light bulb, the room is lit with heat.
The window is the sun's lens, its dusty slice
Of light falls on the woman's foot. The woman
Is my Mother – the clicking of her scissors
Fascinates the little feminine boy
In striped shirt, Tootal tie, thick woollen socks,
His garters down. Memory insists the boy is me.
The house still stands where we stood then.
The inheritance I had, her only child,
Was her party melancholy and a body
Thickening like hers, the wide-pored flesh
Death broke into twenty years ago.

EDWIN BROCK
When My Father Died

On the day my father died
   all the hoops in the neighbourhood rang
   skate wheels shrilled on summer pavements
   and I in my blakey-boots clanged one foot in each gutter

On the day my father died
   girls were running autumn-eyed, with wild hair
   and hands of silk; peg-tops had come round again
   and in the sky the angels were as plain as wings

But on the day my father died
   white faces fell from every window
   and every house found rooms of tears to hide
   while I, joy-jumping, empty eyed sang on the day my father died

Now my father dies a little every day
And the faces from each window grow like mine.

JOHN HARVEY
Apples

My father is dying.
The rain, incessant:
reports of flooding
drift back on the wind.
Scent of apples
from the night stand.
I reach out my hand and rest
one hard against my face;
he taught me how to tell
the real thing from the fake,
hold it close beside the ear
and shake – a genuine Cox,
the seeds will rattle loose
inside their case. You see.

He told me and I swallowed
every word by rote.
Five cotton towns of Lancashire,
five woollen towns, four rivers
that flow into the Wash – Witham,
Welland, Nen and Great Ouse.
Once learned, never forgotten.

My father is dying. He died
nine years ago this June.
They phoned from the hospital
after five with the news.
His face like a cask once used
for storing living things.
A cup of tea, grown cold
and orange on the stand
beside the bed. Did I imagine that?
Length of his fingers, nails like horn,
unclipped. Though dead,
my father is still dying,
a little more each day and slowly,
oh, slowly, sure and slow
as the long fall of rain.
I reach out again for the apple
and bite into its flesh
and hold him bright and sharp,
safe inside the hollow of my mouth.

BRENDAN KENNELLY
A Glimpse of Starlings

I expect him any minute now although
He's dead. I know he has been talking
All night to his own dead and now
In the first heart-breaking light of morning
He is struggling into his clothes,
Sipping a cup of tea, fingering a bit of bread,
Eating a small photograph with his eyes.

The questions bang and rattle in his head
Like doors and cannisters the night of a storm.
He doesn't know why his days finished like this
Daylight is as hard to swallow as food
Love is a crumb all of him hungers for.
I can hear the drag of his feet on the concrete path
The close explosion of his smoker's cough
The slow turn of the Yale key in the lock
The door opening to let him in
To what looks like release from what feels like pain
And over his shoulder a glimpse of starlings
Suddenly lifted over field, road and river
Like a fist of black dust pitched in the wind.

BRENDAN KENNELLY
I See You Dancing, Father

No sooner downstairs after the night's rest
And in the door
Than you started to dance a step
In the middle of the kitchen floor.

And as you danced
You whistled.
You made your own music
Always in tune with yourself.

Well, nearly always, anyway.
You're buried now
In Lislaughtin Abbey
And whenever I think of you

I go back beyond the old man
Mind and body broken
To find the unbroken man.
It is the moment before the dance begins,

Your lips are enjoying themselves
Whistling an air.
Whatever happens or cannot happen
In the time I have to spare
I see you dancing, father.

KEN SMITH
Years Go By

Father I say. Dad? You again?
I take your arm, your elbow,
I turn you round in the dark and I say

go back now, you're sleep walking again,
you're talking out loud again
and your dream is disturbing my dream.

And none of this is your bag of apples,
and even now as the centuries begin to happen
I can say: go away now, you and all your violence.

Shush, now, old man.
Time to go back now to your seat in the one-and-nines,
to your black bench on the Esplanade,

your name and your dates on a brown plate, back
to your own deckchair on the pier, your very own
kitchen chair tipped back on the red kitchen tiles

and you asleep, your feet up on the brass fender
and the fire banked, your cheek cocked
to the wireless, this is the 9 o'clock news Dad.

It's time. It's long past it.
Time to go back up the long pale corridor
there's no coming back from. Ever.

EDNA EGLINTON
Attempts at the Rational Approach

It isn't in important situations
that I miss you.
There is always someone who will help
when the toilet floods
or the tiles blow down.
I've learnt to wire a plug,
put up a shelf, to improvise,
make do, or go without.

I have grown a hardened shell
to wear when walking on my own
into restaurants, theatres,
cinemas and bars.

I have grown accustomed
to causing an odd number,
being partnerless at parties,
disturbing symmetry.

Till suddenly I hear the name
of a place we used to visit –
see a snippet in the paper
about an old-time friend –
think up a silly pun
which you would understand...

I have learnt new thoughts,
new skills, tested new ventures,
found diversion in a dozen
first-time ways...

But when the car-keys disappear
from where I left them,
when next-door's prowling cat
finds an open window,
when the sugarbowl slides off
the kitchen table –
there is no one here to shout at
but myself.

JACK HIRSCHMAN
October 11, 1990

It was a happy day
when he was born
34 years ago
my blond son.

How golden the sun
in the park today,
how happy the birds
and flying balls.

I sit in golden light
almost forgetting
he's eight years gone
because the sun

is so like his hair
and the air like
the golden laughter
of his love.

Eight years old and
into a radiant windup.
Here comes a perfect
strike of light

upon an old old glove.

MICHAEL COADY
Wave and Undertow

1

An inland child, I can remember
the moment I first met
the giant scope of sea,
advancing on my first
communion feet.

Eyelids heavy with horizons
between cool sheets I listened
to the landing clock conspiring
in the rituals of dark, a ship
remotely booming in the harbour.

Above me in the lamplight
gentle fingers of my grandmother
sprinkling holy water on
my face, my whispered words
– *what makes the waves?*

She bent to kiss my forehead –

Almighty God makes waves and men
and light and dark –

and turned down the lamp.

2

The quality of mercy is not strained:
It droppeth as the gentle rain from heaven
Upon the place beneath.

My childheart measured summers
in the haven of her ways –

shutters barred against the dark,
hiss of gaslight over ironing,
milk saucered out to kittens, hands
kneading dough on a scoured table, lips
that quoted Shakespeare like a prayer.

Beside her in the organ loft for Benediction
heady with incense I heard the chant
of the Divine Praises, knew the stop she chose
for *Adoremus in Aeternum*, felt the flooring
tremble with the final diapason.

3

For fifty years the handmaid to this liturgy
of praising, she should have slipped away at last
in innocence and balm of blessed unction.

But when I was grown old enough to think
my eye might hold the measure
of wave and undertow.

some evil thing was born beneath
her porcelain of skin. It swelled
to overwhelm her mind at last,
make her mouth a host to words
that no one could believe
she'd ever use,
and leave her drowning
in a place of locks and fears.

JOHN DUFFY
High Tide

The last time I saw him (I had travelled
from England and the other far places
sons must return from), we went
to witness the Clyde's highest tide
of the century.
                Walking through
the new town's straight lines
of lives laid neatly out –
silver flickers through blinds
the only sign of other life –
we laughed that no one chose to share
the cold dark damp with us.
                I told him
that though we had been the last
in our street to have television,
he'd always taught us how to look
at birds, canal locks, gyroscopes;
the way men use their skills
in ordinary jobs; how to find
excitement in the precision
of an engine or a rose.

He never said how ill he was,
and I was careful not to ask.

Reaching the fields
where we sometimes walked,
we saw the water
spilled across that space, the other bank
pushed far away.
                    The gloom gathered,
we were happy, the power of river
and sea clashing at our feet.
                    The face
of the water was turbulent, something huge
was moving over enormous distances.

MATT SIMPSON
The Ghost of My Mother

What of her history when all the traces
are of him: his hair bunched in the nose,
the excremental wax that clogs my ears,
a moody sea at work in the veins?
Her death alone was memorable,
a blood-burst in the mouth.
She was his victim – much as I
still carting round his blustering ghost
that beat her down. What of her
when I revamp his tantrums
and sudden shamefaced tenderness
that buys back love with promises,
embittered dreams of something good?

Ghosts are rarely charitable.
And now she nudges me,
with frightened, loving eyes.

MATT SIMPSON
Dead Ringer

I've tried, dad, talking you round,
needing your thumbs up. But now
I'm past it and, in any case,
you've been dead too long. It's just
that sometimes at the mirror you
stare through me with something
quizzical that I've no answer to.

Easy for you, you joked your way
out of almost everything. That night
I'm in the bath and you burst in:
'Swap,' you said, 'a tanner and
my owld one for that?'

Still can't get over your lying there
that way. A breathless mirror,
gawping and unfunny mouth.

RUPERT M. LOYDELL
National Railway Museum

I am shadowing
the possibility
of your ghost
in the engine house
I never would have visited
were you here.

I look as though with you –
locos, carriages and models;
breathe in the smuts
of a hundred yard journey
on a working tank engine;
both nostalgic and excited.

252

I look for you:
a son seeking a father
among the iron facts
of the displayed past.
All steamed up
over nothing.

C.K. WILLIAMS
Faint Praise
(for Jim Moss, 1935-1961)

Whatever last slump of flesh
rolls like a tongue in the mouth of your grave,
whatever thin rags of your underwear
are melting in the slow, tiny stomachs,
I am still here; I have survived.

I thought when you died that your angels,
stern, dangerous bats with cameras and laws,
would swarm like bees
and that the silences flaming from you
would fuse me like a stone.

There were no new landscapes I could prepare for you.
I let you go.
And tonight, again, I will eat, read,
and my wife and I will move into love
in the swells of each other like ships.
The loose aerial outside will snap,
the traffic lights blink and change,
the dried lives of autumn crackle like cellophane.

And I will have my life still.
In the darkness, it will lie over against me,
it will whisper, and somehow,
after everything, open to me again.

DAVID H.W. GRUBB
Grandfather's Sermons

Grandfather did not have dust on his words,
they were perfect signals, accurate, cool.
He distrusted the ornate and fabulous,
those small inventions of flattery,
as 'flourishes to fool'.

Setting down his sermons in longhand, he examined
again and again. Searching for miracles in ordinary days
he demonstrated passages to grandmother
inspired by her questions,
only certain of her praise.

When the sermon was over, the hymn announced,
he gathered up his Bible and looked towards her pew.
In that exchange of looks he learnt
if he had been caught-out by glory
or forced by the simple sense of truth.

When we buried him she was too frail to leave her bed.
She heard three hundred letters read aloud, believing three or four.
She stayed with us six weeks longer, silent and white,
then died without his words, his careful texts;
his noise.

BRENDAN CLEARY
Graveside
(for my father)

A graveyard crammed with Protestants & you
all overlooking the knackered cement works

over at Magheramourne. I ride there, borrow Derm's bike
about twice a year & in some awkward phase I'm usually in

I stand & talk to your headstone, not entirely convinced
that you can hear me or that you ever do follow me around;

watch me in my city high-rise stoned, articulate then giggling
when Jo comes over & the sunset looms at Spital Tongues,

or the nights when I chat up pretty English students
in The Strawberry or when I just float about Eldon Square

trying to explain just why the city has taught me endless fear,
& let's say I've had the odd fling, the odd transgression

from the way you wanted me to be. I'm not half as gentle
as you were, nor as caring, but you can appreciate the world's changed!

So I can't keep harking back to that night in 1975
when I sat in with you cos Peg had to go to Bingo.

You asked for tea & toast coated in Lyles Golden Syrup
& it was almost as if you knew the score & felt like

a last small indulgence, a taste of what was perfect.
They came & took you to the coronary unit but I wasn't wakened

& the cardiograph they did was clear but you had them outwitted.
I was sent for in Geography & in the office Nurse Curry looked grave.

I could replay the whole scene at random & have done
& the last words I'd written in the classroom were 'broken marriages'

& Peg told me that my future plans should stay exactly the same
& I thought that was justice, I've never regretted it.

I'll never be completely English, I hope you must know that
& I do strive to be as gentle & as considerate –

at least when I blow it, get tainted by Black Bush & urges
at least I agonise over it. So if you can hear me

I'd like it if you were always nearby watching.
I've never forgotten my brother's face when Peg went to tell him.

He drew up in his Post van & she reached out to hug him.
& how I saw how his face twisted, from up in the top room.

That's imprinted on me wherever I go, this year Europe,
next year The States, today the graveside at Islandmagee.

I'm a few steps behind you, but I'm catching up...

LES MURRAY
The Steel
*(in memory of my mother, Miriam Murray née Arnall,
born 23.5.1915, died 19.4.1951)*

I am older than my mother.
Cold steel hurried me from her womb.
I haven't got a star.

What hour I followed
the waters into this world
no one living can now say.
My zodiac got washed away.

The steel of my induction
killed my brothers and sisters;
once or twice I was readied for them

and then they were not mentioned
again, at the hospital
to me or to the visitors.
The reticence left me only.

I think, apart from this,
my parents' life was happy,
provisional, as lives are.

Farming spared them from the war,
that and an ill-knit blue shin
my father had been harried back

to tree-felling with, by his father
who supervised from horseback.
The times were late pioneer.

So was our bare plank house
with its rain stains down each crack
like tall tan flames,
magic swords, far matched perspectives:

it reaped Dad's shamed invectives –
Paying him rent for this shack!
The landlord was his father.

But we also had fireside ease,
health, plentiful dinners, the radio;
we'd a car to drive to tennis.

Country people have cars
for more than shopping and show,
our Dodge reached voting age, though,
in my first high school year.

I was in the town at school
the afternoon my mother
collapsed, and was carried from the dairy.
The car was out of order.

The ambulance was available
but it took a doctor's say-so
to come. This was refused.
My father pleaded. Was refused.

The local teacher's car was got finally.
The time all this took didn't pass,
it spread through sheets, unstoppable.

Thirty-seven miles to town
and the terrible delay.
Little blood brother, blood sister,
I don't blame you.
How can you blame a baby?
or the longing for a baby?

Little of that week
comes back. The vertigo,
the apparent recovery –
She will get better now.
The relapse on the Thursday.

In school and called away
I was haunted, all that week,
by the spectre of dark women,
Murrays dressed in midday black

who lived on the river islands
and are seen only at funerals;
their terrible weak authority.

Everybody in the town
was asking me about my mother;
I could only answer childishly
to them. And to my mother,

and on Friday afternoon
our family world
went inside itself forever.

Sister Arnall, city girl
with your curt good sense,
were you being the nurse
when you let them hurry me?
being responsible

when I was brought on to make way
for a difficult birth in that cottage hospital
and the Cheers child stole my birthday?

Or was it our strange diffidence,
unworldly at a pinch, unresentful,
being a case among cases,

a relative, wartime sense,
modern, alien to fuss,
that is not in the Murrays?

I don't blame the Cheers boy's mother:
she didn't put her case.
It was the steel proposed
reasonably, professionally,
that became your sentence

but I don't decry unselfishness:
I'm proud of it. Of you.
Any virtue can be fatal.

In the event, his coming gave no trouble
but it might have, I agree;
nothing you agreed to harmed me.
I didn't mean to harm you
I was a baby.

For a long time, my father
himself became a baby
being perhaps wiser than me,
less modern, less military;

he was not ashamed of grief,
of its looking like a birth
out through the face

bloated, whiskery, bringing no relief.
It was mainly through fear
that I was at times his father.
I have long been sorry.

Caked pans, rancid blankets,
despair and childish cool
were our road to Bohemia
that bitter wartime country.

What were you thinking of,
Doctor MB, BS?
Were you very tired?
Did you have more pressing cases?

Know panic when you heard it:
Oh you can bring her in!
Did you often do
diagnosis by telephone?

Perhaps we wrong you,
make a scapegoat of you;
perhaps there was no stain
of class in your decision,

no view that two framed degrees
outweighed a dairy.
It's nothing, dear:
just some excited hillbilly –

As your practice disappeared
and you were cold-shouldered in town
till you broke and fled,
did you think of the word *Clan?*

It is an antique
concept. But not wholly romantic.
We came to the river early;
it gives us some protection.

You'll agree the need is real.
I can forgive you now
and not to seem magnanimous.
It's enough that you blundered
on our family steel.

Thirty-five years on earth:
that's short. That's short, Mother,
as the lives cut off by war

and the lives of spilt children are short.
Justice wholly in this world
would bring them no rebirth
nor restore your latter birthdays.
How could that be justice?

My father never quite
remarried. He went back
by stages of kindness to me
to the age of lonely men,
of only men, and men's company

that is called the Pioneer age.
Snig chain and mountain track;
he went back to felling trees

and seeking justice from his
dead father. His only weakness.
One's life is not a case

except of course it is.
Being just, seeking justice:
they were both of them right,
my mother and my father.

There is justice, there is death,
humanist: you can't have both.
Activist, you can't serve both.
You do not move in measured space.

The poor man's anger is a prayer
for equities Time cannot hold
and steel grows from our mother's grace.
Justice is the people's otherworld.

ANTHONY RUDOLF
Old Man
(Joseph Rudolf, born 30 November 1880, died 2 September 1980)

Old man, you governed
my life.
        I wanted
to write you,
            your life.

What for?
      Who for?
My daughter's daughter?
Your seed unto?
Oh, you did well
to leave,
      who knew
nothing of the thousand
suns of the bomb.
Less light.
      Less
light.
   No more
poems; and what
returns
for our pains;
      sleep
Joseph, sleep,
      face up,
lad's love.

PABLO NERUDA
The More-Mother
(translated from the Spanish by Alastair Reid)

My more-mother comes by
in her wooden shoes. Last night
the wind blew from the pole, the roof tiles
broke, and walls
and bridges fell.
The pumas of night howled all night long,
and now, in the morning
of icy sun, she comes,
my more-mother, Dona
Trinidad Marverde,
soft as the tentative freshness
of the sun in storm country,
a frail lamp, self-effacing,
lighting up
to show others the way.

Dear more-mother –
I was never able
to say stepmother! –
at this moment
my mouth trembles to define you,
for hardly
had I begun to understand
than I saw goodness in poor dark clothes,
a practical sanctity –
goodness of water and flour,
that's what you were. Life made you into bread,
and there we fed on you,
long winter to forlorn winter
with raindrops leaking
inside-the house,
and you,
ever present in your humility,
sifting
the bitter
grain-seed of poverty
as if you were engaged in
sharing out
a river of diamonds.

Oh, mother, how could I
not go on remembering you
in every living minute?
Impossible. I carry
your Marverde in my blood,
surname
of the shared bread,
of those gentle hands
which shaped from a flour sack
my childhood clothes,
of the one who cooked, ironed, washed,
planted, soothed fevers,
and when everything was done
and I at last was able
to stand on my own sore feet,
she went off, fulfilled, dark,
off in her small coffin
where for once she was idle
under the hard rain of Temuca.

PABLO NERUDA
The Father
(translated from the Spanish by Alastair Reid)

My blunt father comes back
from the trains.
We recognise
in the night
the whistle
of the locomotive
perforating the rain
with a wandering moan,
lament of the night,
and later
the door shivering open.
A rush of wind
came in with my father,
and between footsteps and drafts
the house
shook,
the surprised doors
banged with the dry
bark of pistols,
the staircase groaned,
and a loud voice,
complaining, grumbled
while the wild dark,
the waterfall rain
rumbled on the roofs
and, little by little,
drowned the world
and all that could be heard was the wind
battling with the rain.

He was, however, a daily happening.
Captain of his train, of the cold dawn,
and scarcely had the sun
begun to show itself
than there he was with his beard,
his red and green
flags, his lamps prepared,
the engine coal in its little inferno,

the station with trains in the mist,
and his duty to geography.
The railwayman is a sailor on earth
and in the small ports without a sea line –
the forest towns – the train runs, runs,
unbridling the natural world,
completing its navigation of the earth.
When the long train comes to rest,
friends come together,
come in, and the doors of my childhood open,
the table shakes
at the slam of a railwayman's hand,
the thick glasses of companions jump
and the glitter
flashes out
from the eyes of the wine.

My poor, hard father,
there he was at the axis of existence,
virile in friendship, his glass full.
His life was a running campaign,
and between his early risings and his traveling,
between arriving and rushing off,
one day, rainier than other days,
the railwayman, José del Carmen Reyes,
climbed aboard the train of death and so far has not come back.

TONY FLYNN
A Mother's Death

Night, and your frail
plants exhaust our air.
                        In the washing-basket
soiled clothes accumulate.
Soon they will spill
into the room
and life will begin again –
they will wash their own socks.

AILEEN CAMPBELL
The Smile
(for Aunt M)

She permeated the old house with an impersonal air
like the whiff of paraffin from a host of lamps lit at dusk
then left on ledges by stairways and in spooky recesses of the halls.
In rooms gas mantles popped and hissed, where she stitched –
one time a cover made from cast-offs and rick-rack braid.
We'd lie in bed remembering, both pointing out the patchwork
      past...
this bit my blouse, that bit your dress and there a square of her
      apron.
Her pantry was haphazard; scones, plums, tuberous potatoes,
bottles, books, half-open packets. When we stole food nothing was
      said.
Mice were also tolerated.
Our family house gave space to more aunts, uncles, a
grannie, but she was the unobtrusive one, keeping her conscience
      in its place,
creating untidy comfort, though dust disappeared, floors stayed
      waxed
while a fire burned in the wash-house, that den of spell and
      alchemy –
the smoke, the steam, the inferno below a cracked stone boiler
where crystals and powders transformed our muddy clothes.
We did not need to look for gold in the cold ash at the finish.
The ancient mangle with cog wheels wrung out the dark, and
      shining things
were pegged beside sunflowers. Garden and home were her
      entirety.
The world of streets and news was beyond her magic ring.
She could grow anything. Bare earth would quicken at her glance
      and bloom
(or so it seemed in our childhood).

JOHN HAINES
To Vera Thompson

Woman whose face
is a blurred map of roots,
I might be buried here
and you dreaming in the warmth
of this late northern summer.

Say I was the last
soldier on the Yukon,
my war fought out
with leaves and thorns.

Here is the field;
it lies thick with horsetail,
fireweed, and stubborn rose.
The wagons and stables
followed the troopers
deep into soil and smoke.
When a summer visitor
steps over the rotting sill
the barracks floor
thumps with a hollow sound.

Life and death grow quieter
and lonelier here by the river.
Summer and winter
the town sleeps and settles,
history is no more than sunlight
on a weathered cross.

The picket fence sinks
to a row of mossy shadows,
the gate locks with a rusty pin.
Stand there now
and say that you loved me,
that I will not be forgotten
when a ghostwind
drifts through the canyon
and our years grow deep
in a snow of roses and stones.

JOHN BERRYMAN
from **Dream Songs**

384

The marker slants, flowerless, day's almost done,
I stand above my father's grave with rage,
often, often before
I've made this awful pilgrimage to one
who cannot visit me, who tore his page
out: I come back for more,

I spit upon this dreadful banker's grave
who shot his heart out in a Florida dawn
O ho alas alas
When will indifference come, I moan & rave
I'd like to scrabble till I got right down
away down under the grass

and ax the casket open ha to see
just how he's taking it, which he sought so hard
we'll tear apart
the mouldering grave clothes ha & then Henry
will heft the ax once more, his final card,
and fell it on the start.

ROBERT PACK
Father

I have not needed you for thirteen years.
You left my mother to me like a bride.
To take your place, I shut off all my tears,
And with your death, it was my grief that died.
How could I know that women worship pain?
My mother's eyes bring back your ghost again.

I dreamed that digging in the humid ground
You found, among the worms, my embryo;
You put it on a hook – it made no sound
Opening its mouth as you let it go
Into the lake where, fishing from a boat,
You watched the bulging, blood-eyed fishes float.

Falling, the strong at least learn gentleness.
When you cried out – that was your mastery!
I took a wife, but never let her guess
It was your ghost that chose my secrecy.
She needed what you would not have me show:
My need. Your strength too late let weakness grow.

I dreamed we both rowed through a windy mist;
The dark lake tilted where you wished to go.
Fish scales and blood glowed at me from your wrist;
The air I gulped only the drowning know.
You had me hold the net, and I believed
The fish's spastic death was what I grieved.

Screams come too easily these guarded days.
The bright, complaining, are most eloquent.
Must loss always be prelude to our praise?
Is this what mother's rising mourning meant?
For whose sake did I envy suicide?
Could death win wife and mother as one bride?

I dreamed you threw the unhooked fish away.
Why did I fear I had done something wrong?
You took me home, insisting that I stay,
But I did not feel weak, feeling you strong,
For when you left I found the net behind,
And angered as gored waters gagged my mind.

I have not needed you for thirteen years.
I have grown grim with my authority.
Take back my mother and release my tears,
And let a child's lost grief give strength to me!
Dreaming, I seek your skeleton below;
I dig the worms and find your embryo.

LOTTE KRAMER
A Dramatist Who Was My Father

All day, on Sundays,
He walked in the woods, alone,
Needing exhaustion.

The mushroom silence
Of trees tuned his voice,
The sudden brightness

Of meadows glazed
And bandaged his icon-wounds
Of unwritten words.

At home, old manuscripts
Yellowed and mourned in dense
Drawers of his desk;

But still new lines
That would never smell ink
Or paper breathed

Their last upright
Declensions on a stage-set
Of queues and gas,

His words, now ashes,
Bitter, perpetual powder
On my tongue.

JAMES BERRY
Thoughts on My Father

You are boned clean now.
You are lost like dice and teeth.
Don't bother knock
I won't represent you.

A sound brain you were,
your body a mastery,
but no turning into any stepping stone
or handing anybody a key.

Simply it hurts that needing
we offended you
and I judge you by lack.

Playing some well shaped shadow
the sun alone moved,
you wouldn't be mixed with cash
or the world's cunning.

So perfectly exclusive,
you tantalised me.
You split our home in passions.
Every year we were more blunted.

I knew nowhere.
My eyes looked out from you
my first god.

Omnipotence breathed
come boy come
to hungrybelly revelations.

Lift your hat to doom
boy in the manner that roadside
weeds are indestructible.

Stubborn tides you echo.

I moved your sterile tones
from my voice.
I lifted your mole
from my back.

You scar me man,
but I must go over you again and again.
I must plunge my raging eyes
in all your steady enduring.

I must assemble material
of my own
for a new history.

FRANCES WILSON
Botticelli Baby
(a postcard to my mother)

Mother, this one's for you.
Not the usual pastoral
back-drop, this inner city yard,
but the sun's pure Umbrian
and the street beyond with slopes
of rooftops, lines of washing,
is an exercise in perspective.

Look at the gold-leaf burnish
on the dark hair of the sun-browned
woman, her face a perfect oval;
bare-footed, black skirt
hitched up above her knees,
she sweeps the stones between
her pots of basil, bay, geraniums.

I'm sitting on the top step
stringing beans, thinking of you,
wishing you knew how much more often
since you died, I get in touch.

Remembering – missing now –
your English awkwardness,
how bad you were at kissing,

how you disliked garlic, mistrusted
herbs and music. Anything operatic
was beyond your repertoire. You
couldn't have been less Latin. And yet
you'd drop your maiden name *Tarelli*
into conversations with the proud
deliberate frequency of a lover's.

Look where your lineage has reached.
See how your grand-daughter props
up her broom, loosens her skirt,
stoops and scoops from beneath
the fennel's feathery shadow
her plump and dimpled baby,
Italian as any Botticelli cherub.

U.A. FANTHORPE
Fanfare
*(for Winifrid Fanthorpe,
born 5 Februry 1895, died 13 November 1978)*

You, in the old photographs, are always
The one with the melancholy half-smile, the one
Who couldn't quite relax into the joke.

My extrovert dog of a father,
With his ragtime blazer and his swimming togs
Tucked like a swiss roll under his arm,
Strides in his youth towards us down some esplanade,

Happy as Larry. You, on his other arm,
Are anxious about the weather forecast,
His overdraft, or early closing day.

You were good at predicting failure: marriages
Turned out wrong because you said they would.
You knew the rotations of armistice and war,
Watched politicians' fates with gloomy approval.

All your life you lived in a minefield,
And were pleased, in a quiet way, when mines
Exploded. You never actually said
I told you so, but we could tell you meant it.

Crisis was your element. You kept your funny stories
Your music-hall songs for doodlebug and blitz-nights.
In the next cubicle, after a car-crash, I heard you
Amusing the nurses with your trench wit through the blood.

Magic alerted you. Green, knives and ladders
Will always scare me through your tabus.
Your nightmare was Christmas; so much organised
Compulsory whoopee to be got through.

You always had some stratagem for making
Happiness keep its distance. Disaster
Was what you planned for. You always
Had hoarded loaves or candles up your sleeve.

Houses crumbled around your ears, taps leaked,
Electric light bulbs went out all over England,
Because for you homes were only provisional,
Bivouacs on the stony mountain of living.

You were best at friendship with chars, gypsies,
Or very far-off foreigners. Well-meaning neighbours
Were dangerous because they lived near.

Me too you managed best at a distance. On the landline
From your dugout to mine, your nightly
Pass, friend was really often quite jovial.

You were the lonely figure in the doorway
Waving goodbye in the cold, going back to a sink-full
Of crockey dirtied by those you loved. We
Left you behind to deal with our crusts and gristle.

I know why you chose now to die. You foresaw
Us approaching the Delectable Mountains,
And didn't feel up to all the cheers and mafficking.

But how, dearest, will even you retain your
Special brand of hard-bitten stoicism
Among the halleluyas of the triumphant dead?

ANDREW SALKEY
Clearsightedness
(in memory of Claudia Jones)

In spite of what the quarrymen said,
she was sure she knew only too well
that she was born to see through stone,
to slash that broad back with her eyes
and tell her daughter about it, one day.

I remember we'd often catch her smiling,
brushing rock-dust out of her hair,
clapping her granite-veined hands,
slapping her long skirt with carpet-clatter,
and looking like a moving hive of hillside.

'I'm every bit as hard as they hit me,'
she liked saying, winking confidently.
'Remember, we live on a rock in water,
nothing surprises me, only my eyes.
I can see us striking back. I can see it.'

ELAINE FEINSTEIN
Dad

Your old hat hurts me, and those black
    fat raisins you liked to press into
my palm from your soft heavy hand.
    I see you staggering back up the path
with sacks of potatoes from some local farm,
    fresh eggs, flowers. Every day I grieve

for your great heart broken and you gone.
    You loved to watch the trees. This year
you did not see their Spring.
    The sky was freezing over the fen
as on that somewhere secretly appointed day
    you beached: cold, white-faced, shivering.

What happened, old bull, my loyal
    hoarse-voiced warrior? The hammer
blow that stopped you in your track
    and brought you to a hospital monitor
could not destroy your courage
    to the end you were
uncowed and unconcerned with pleasing anyone.

I think of you now as once again safely
    at my mother's side, the earth as
chosen as a bed, and feel most sorrow for
    all that was gentle in
my childhood buried there
    already forfeit, now forever lost.

W.S. GRAHAM
Lines on Roger Hilton's Watch

Which I was given because
I loved him and we had
Terrible times together.

O tarnished ticking time
Piece with your bent hand,
You must be used to being
Looked at suddenly
In the middle of the night
When he switched the light on
Beside his bed. I hope
You told him the best time
When he lifted you up
To meet the Hilton gaze.

I lift you up from the mantel
Piece here in my house
Wearing your verdigris.
At least I keep you wound
And put my ear to you
To hear Botallack tick.

You realise your master
Has relinquished you
And gone to lie under
The ground at St Just.

Tell me the time. The time
Is Botallack o'clock.
This is the dead of night.

He switches the light on
To find a cigarette
And pours himself a Teachers.
He picks me up and holds me
Near his lonely face
To see my hands. He thinks
He is not being watched.

The images of his dream
Are still about his face
As he spits and tries not
To remember where he was.

I am only a watch
And pray time hastes away.
I think I am running down.

Watch, it is time I wound
You up again. I am
Very much not your dear
Last master but we had
Terrible times together.

LAWRENCE DURRELL
Father Nicholas His Death: Corfu

Hush the old bones their vegetable sleep,
For the islands will never grow old.
Nor like Atlantis on a Monday tumble,
Struck like soft gongs in the amazing blue.

Dip the skull's chinks in lichens and sleep,
Old man, beside the water-gentry.
The hero standing knee-deep in his dreams
Will find and bind the name upon his atlas,
And put beside it only an X marked spot.

Leave memory to the two tall sons and lie
Calmed in smiles by the elegiac blue.
A man's address to God is the skeleton's humour,
A music sipped by the flowers.

Consider please the continuous nature of Love:
How one man dying and another smiling.
Conserve for the maggot only a seed of pity,
As in winter's taciturn womb we see already
A small and woollen lamb on a hilltop hopping.

The dying and the becoming are one thing,
So wherever you go the musical always is;
Now what are your pains to the Great Danube's pains,
Your pyramids of despair against Ithaca
Or the underground rivers of Dis?

Your innocence shall be as the clear cistern
Where the lone animal in these odourless waters
Quaffs at his own reflection a shining ink.
Here at your green pasture the old psalms
Shall kneel like humble brutes and drink.

Hush then the finger bones their mineral doze
For the islands will never be old or cold
Nor ever the less blue: for the egg of beauty
Blossoms in new migrations, the whale's grey acres,
For men of the labyrinth of the dream of death.
So sleep.
All these warm when the flesh is cold.
And the blue will keep.

LEE HARWOOD
African Violets
(for Pansy Harwood, my grandmother, 1896-1989)

Flags stream from the tops of the silver pyramids
Purple flowers present themselves to the air, the world
Chopin fights his way through all the notes, the choices

All this, and yet that emptiness

A real heart-breaker, tears in my eyes

What did I give you? At the last a pot of flowers,
your favourite colour, you said
then died soon after, the day after
I'd left you there in the bare hospital room
your eyes and voice so clear in the recognition
like so many years before   'O Travers'

And you gave me? everything I know.

But to reduce this to yet another poem
to entertain

pages of words creating old routines

I systematically smash all those pretty pictures,
they won't do anymore.
'That was a bit unnecessary, son,' you say.
I know, but their weight does you no service.

My blood is your blood,
it's as ancient as that;
pride and style that you had,
and with all a lovely generosity
I treasure.

I find myself moving as you would,
not the same but similar,
sharing your tastes and paths;
the night jasmine bower.

The strength of these memories
The comfort your home was

Yet it seems almost another world –
building rabbit hutches on winter evenings
in your living room, sawdust and
wood shavings on the worn carpet, easily cleared.
A house that was lived in, not exhibited.

And all those other evenings, summer or winter,
spent pickling onions, or bottling fruit,
or wrapping boxes of apples for store,
or stringing onions to hang in the shed
above the sacked potatoes,
or mending our own shoes,
all the work, cooking, making,
fixing, all done capably, easily
together.

But you now gone forever

Not sat in the corner of the couch
after your morning bath, with a cup of tea
reading the morning paper.
That ritual finished

though other 'stuff' continues
as your blood continues to flow in me
no matter what I might say
(the tense continually shifts, past and present blur)
we both love(d) love and were, are natural liars,
easy with the 'truth', turning facts to meet the story;
we both have a distaste for 'trade' –
all the contradictions happily ignored;
we both…

Now wandering helpless around my room
the rich world about,
the flags and skies, the dreams

I talk to you again and again,
I see you again and again   sat there

JAMES BROCKWAY
As Once…

We can live without the ones we loved
and lost,
those we shall love forever.

Observe this woman:
for years she nursed
an ailing father.

Lost him, buried him.

Look at this snap a while –
how radiant her smile.

Then her companion:
for years she tended her
paradise in vain.

Lost him, buried him.

Look now – her laugh
fills half the photograph.

*

I mourn you too in secret –
lifting only one glass down
to mix a drink.

Finding you as I turn
no longer there,
greeting mere air.

Suddenly, in a museum,
trapped by a Renoir,

forever on the brink.

Feeling the Mediterranean sun
explore my skin again,
as once...

As once.

TESS GALLAGHER
Infinite Room

Having lost future with him
I'm fit now to love those
who offer no future when future
is the heart's way of throwing itself away
in time. He gave me all, even
the last marbled instant, and not as excess,
but as if a closed intention were itself
a spring by the roadside
I could put my lips to and be quenched
remembering. So love in a room now
can too easily make me lost
like a child having to hurry home
in darkness, afraid the house
will be empty. Or just afraid.

Tell me again how this is only
for as long as it lasts. I want to be
fragile and true as one who extends
the moment with its death intact,
with her too wise heart
cleansed of that debris we called hope.
Only then can I revisit that last surviving
and know with the wild exactness
of a shattered window what he meant
with all time gone
when he said, 'I love you.'

Now offer me again
what you thought was nothing.

ELIZABETH JENNINGS
Into the Hour

I have come into the hour of a white healing.
Grief's surgery is over and I wear
The scar of my remorse and of my feeling.

I have come into a sudden sunlit hour
When ghosts are scared to corners. I have come
Into the time when grief begins to flower

Into a new love. It had filled my room
Long before I recognised it. Now
I speak its name. Grief finds its good way home.

The apple-blossom's handsome on the bough
And Paradise spreads round. I touch its grass.
I want to celebrate but don't know how.

I need not speak though everyone I pass
Stares at me kindly. I would put my hand
Into their hands. Now I have lost my loss

In some way I may later understand.
I hear the singing of the summer grass.
And love, I find, has no considered end,

Nor is it subject to the wilderness
Which follows death. I am not traitor to
A person or a memory. I trace

Behind that love another which is running
Around, ahead. I need not ask its meaning.

ELEANOR MAXTED
Moving On

The eighth spring has come early:
the dog put up a rabbit on his walk
but chased it without malice, then forgot it.
We are all one year older.

The cat sunbathes inside his shadow,
the house is tidier, the garden fatter.
Books deliberate on death and grief,
they are one year older: they repeat themselves.

And if I rejoin your letters
they have grown stiffer,
and your voice is farther off
like someone talking through a closed door.

EMILY BRONTË
Remembrance

Cold in the earth – and the deep snow piled above thee,
Far, far removed, cold in the dreary grave!
Have I forgot, my only Love, to love thee,
Severed at last by Time's all-severing wave?

Now, when alone, do my thoughts no longer hover
Over the mountains, on that northern shore,
Resting their wings where heath and fern-leaves cover
Thy noble heart for ever, ever more?

Cold in the earth – and fifteen wild Decembers
From those brown hills have melted into spring:
Faithful, indeed, is the spirit that remembers
After such years of change and suffering!

Sweet Love of youth, forgive, if I forget thee,
While the world's tide is bearing me along;
Other desires and other hopes beset me,
Hopes which obscure, but cannot do thee wrong!

No later light has lightened up my heaven,
No second morn has ever shone for me;
All my life's bliss from thy dear life was given,
All my life's bliss is in the grave with thee.

But, when the days of golden dreams had perished,
And even Despair was powerless to destroy;
Then did I learn how existence could be cherished,
Strengthened, and fed without the aid of joy.

Then did I check the tears of useless passion –
Weaned my young soul from yearning after thine;
Sternly denied its burning wish to hasten
Down to that tomb already more than mine.

And even yet, I dare not let it languish,
Dare not indulge in memory's rapturous pain;
Once drinking deep of that divinest anguish,
How could I seek the empty world again?

VII. Someone is dressing up
for death today, a change
of skirt or tie...

DENNIS O'DRISCOLL
Someone

someone is dressing up for death today, a change of skirt or tie
eating a final feast of buttered sliced pan, tea
scarcely having noticed the erection that was his last
shaving his face to marble for the icy laying out
spraying with deodorant her coarse armpit grass
someone today is leaving home on business
saluting, terminally, the neighbours who will join in the cortège
someone is trimming his nails for the last time, a precious moment
someone's thighs will not be streaked with elastic in the future
someone is putting out milkbottles for a day that will not come
someone's fresh breath is about to be taken clean away
someone is writing a cheque that will be marked 'drawer deceased'
someone is circling posthumous dates on a calendar
someone is listening to an irrelevant weather forecast
someone is making rash promises to friends
someone's coffin is being sanded, laminated, shined
who feels this morning quite as well as ever
someone if asked would find nothing remarkable in today's date
perfume and goodbyes her final will and testament
someone today is seeing the world for the last time
as innocently as he had seen it first

CAROL ANN DUFFY
Practising Being Dead

Your own ghost, you stand in dark rain
and light aches out from the windows
to lie in pools at your feet. This is the place.
Those are the big oak doors. Behind them
a waxed floor stretches away, backwards
down a corridor of years. The trees sigh.
You are both watching and remembering. Neither.

Inside, the past is the scent of candles the moment
they go out. You saw her, ancient and yellow,
laid out inside that alcove at the stairhead,
a broken string of water on her brow.
For weeks the game was Practising Being Dead,
hands in the praying position, eyes closed, lips
pressed to the colour of sellotape over the breath.

It is accidental and unbearable to recall that time,
neither bitter nor sweet but gone, the future
already lost as you open door after door, each one
peeling back a sepia room empty of promise.
This evening the sky has not enough moon
to give you a shadow. Nobody hears
your footsteps walking away along the gravel drive.

STERLING A. BROWN
Sister Lou

Honey
When de man
Calls out de las' train
You're gonna ride,
Tell him howdy.

Gather up yo' basket
An' yo' knittin' an yo' things,
An' go on up an' visit
Wid frien' Jesus fo' a spell.

Show Marfa
How to make yo' greengrape jellies,
An' give po' Lazarus
A passel of them Golden Biscuits.

Scald some meal
Fo' some rightdown good spoonbread
Fo' li'l box-plunkin' David.

An' sit aroun'
An' tell them Hebrew Chillen
All yo' stories...

Honey
Don't be feared of them pearly gates,
Don't go 'round to de back,
No mo' dataway
Not evah no mo'.

Let Michael tote yo' burden
An' yo' pocketbook an' evah thing
'Cept yo' Bible,
While Gabriel blows somp'n
Solemn but loudsome
On dat horn of his'n.

Honey
Go Straight on to de Big House,
An' speak to yo' God
Without no fear an' tremblin'.

Then sit down
An' pass de time of day awhile.

Give a good talkin' to
To yo' favorite 'postle Peter,
An' rub the po' head
Of mixed-up Judas,
An' joke awhile wid Jonah.

Then, when you gits de chance,
Always rememberin' yo' raisin',
Let 'em know youse tired,
Jest a mite tired.

Jesus will find yo' bed fo' you
Won't no servant evah bother wid yo' room.
Jesus will lead you
To a room wid windows
Openin' on cherry trees an' plum trees
Bloomin' everlastin'.

An' dat will be yours
Fo' keeps.

MILNER PLACE
Last Will and Testament
(in memory of Anna Fissler)

I leave you my breath, cantankerous
bones, various organs; to sleep
in the shade of willows, in a warm bed
among ships.

I bequeath a blunt knife, threads
of unravelled string, nets, pointed
stakes, untended acres, the scent
of almonds.

I adjure you not to forget the picnic
basket, and when you come to me with full arms,
bring a sprig of thyme, a bell full of grapes,
a gentle horse.

FEYYAZ FERGAR
Testament
(for David Perman)

There is no bad blood between death and me.
He can lay claim to my perishable goods,
my dust, my mistakes, my birthdays.

But when I die I shall leave behind
all the tools of my breath.
I shall leave behind
my eyes, my hands,
the results of my voice,
the roads that lived in my veins,
my habit of smuggling windows into houses
under stark arrest.
I shall also leave behind
the light that stood by me
against the sarcasms of the dark.

With all these I shall speak
for the sun.
Turn your cemeteries off!
There is more to come.

DAVID WRIGHT
A Funeral Oration

Composed at thirty, my funeral oration: Here lies
David John Murray Wright, 6'2", myopic blue eyes;
Hair grey (very distinguished looking, so I am told);
Shabbily dressed as a rule; susceptible to cold;
Acquainted with what are known as the normal vices;
Perpetually short of cash; useless in a crisis;
Preferring cats, hated dogs; drank (when he could) too much;
Was deaf as a tombstone; and extremely hard to touch.
Academic achievements: B.A., Oxon (2nd class);
Poetic: the publication of one volume of verse,
Which in his thirtieth year attained him no fame at all
Except among intractable poets, and a small
Lunatic fringe congregating in Soho pubs.
He could roll himself cigarettes from discarded stubs,
Assume the first position of Yoga; sail, row, swim;
And though deaf, in church appear to be joining a hymn.
Often arrested for being without a permit,
Starved on his talents as much as he dined on his wit,
Born in a dominion to which he hoped not to go back
Since predisposed to imagine white possibly black:
His life, like his times, was appalling; his conduct odd;
He hoped to write one good line; died believing in God.

MARK STRAND
My Death

Sadness, of course, and confusion.
The relatives gathered at the graveside,
talking about the waste, and the weather mounting,
the rain moving in vague pillars offshore.

This is Prince Edward Island.
I came back to my birthplace to announce my death.
I said I would ride full gallop into the sea
and not look back. People were furious.

I told them about attempts I had made in the past,
how I starved in order to be the size of Lucille,
whom I loved, to inhabit the cold space
her body had taken. They were shocked.

I went on about the time
I dove in a perfect arc that filled
with the sunshine of farewell and I fell
head over shoulders into the river's thigh.

And about the time
I stood naked in the snow, pointing a pistol
between my eyes, and how when I fired my head bloomed
into health. Soon I was alone.

Now I lie in the box
of my making while the weather
builds and the mourners shake their heads as if
to write or to die, I did not have to do either.

ANONYMOUS *
'Do not stand at my grave and weep'

Do not stand at my grave and weep;
I am not there. I do not sleep.
I am a thousand winds that blow.
I am the diamond glints on snow.
I am the sunlight on ripened grain.
I am the gentle autumn rain.
When you awaken in the morning's hush
I am the swift uplifting rush
Of quiet birds in circled flight.
I am the soft stars that shine at night.
Do not stand at my grave and cry;
I am not there. I did not die.

* Written at least fifty years ago, this poem has been attributed,
at different times, to J.T. Wiggins, Mary E. Fry and Marianne
Reinhardt, and recently to a British soldier killed in Northern
Ireland, Stephen Cummins (who left a copy for his relatives).

GRACE NICHOLS
Tropical Death

The fat black woman want
a brilliant tropical death
not a cold sojourn
in some North Europe far/forlorn

The fat black woman want
some heat/hibiscus at her feet
blue sea dress
to wrap her neat

The fat black woman want
some bawl
no quiet jerk tear wiping
a polite hearse withdrawal

The fat black woman want
all her dead rights
first night
third night
nine night
all the sleepless droning
red-eyed wake nights

In the heart
of her mother's sweetbreast
In the shade
of the sun leaf's cool bless
In the bloom
of her people's bloodrest

the fat black woman want
a brilliant tropical death yes

CÉSAR VALLEJO
Black Stone Lying on a White Stone
(translated from the Spanish by Robert Bly & John Knoepfle)

I will die in Paris, on a rainy day,
on some day which I can already remember.
I will die in Paris – and I do not step aside –
perhaps on a Thursday, as today is Thursday, in autumn

It will be a Thursday, because today, Thursday, setting down
these lines, I have set my shoulder against
the evil, and never so much as today have I found myself
with all the road ahead of me, alone.

César Vallejo is dead. Everyone beat him,
although he never does anything to them;
they beat him hard with a stick and hard also

with a rope. These are the witnesses:
the Thursdays, and the bones of my shoulders,
the solitude, and the rain, and the roads . . .

HANS MAGNUS ENZENSBERGER
Last Will and Testament
(translated from the German by Jerome Rothenberg)

get your flag out of my face, it tickles!
bury my cat inside, bury her over there,
where my chromatic garden used to be!

and get that tinny wreath off my chest, it's rattling too much;
toss it over to the statues on the garbage heap,
and give the ribbon to some biddies to doll themselves up.

say your prayers over the telephone, but first cut the wires,
or wrap them up in a handkerchief full of bread-crumbs
for the stupid fish in the puddles.

let the bishop stay at home and get plastered!
give him a barrel of rum,
he's going to be dry from the sermon.

and get off my back with your tombstones and stovepipe hats!
use the fancy marble to pave an alley where nobody lives,
an alley for pigeons.

my suitcase is full of scribbled pieces of paper for my little cousin,
who can fold them into airplanes, fancy ones for sailing off the
        bridge
so they drown in the river.

anything that's left (a pair of drawers a lighter a fancy birthstone
and an alarm clock) I want you to give callisthenes the junk man
and toss in a fat tip.

as for resurrection of the flesh however and life everlasting
I will, if it's all the same to you, take care of that on my own;
it's my affair, after all. Live and be well!

there's a couple of butts left on the dresser.

PAUL LAURENCE DUNBAR
A Death Song

Lay me down beneaf de willers in de grass,
Whah de branch 'll go a-singin' as it pass.
   An' w'en I's a-layin' low,
   I kin hyeah it as it go
Singin', 'Sleep, my honey, tek yo' res' at las'.'

Lay me nigh to whah hit meks a little pool,
An' de watah stan's so quiet lak an' cool,
   Whah de little birds in spring,
   Ust to come an' drink an' sing,
An' de chillen waded on dey way to school.

Let me settle w'en my shouldahs draps dey load
Nigh enough to hyeah de noises in de road;
   Fu' I t'ink de las' long res'
   Gwine to soothe my sperrit bes'
Ef I's layin' 'mong de t'ings I's allus knowed.

FEDERICO GARCÍA LORCA
Gacela of the Dark Death
(translated from the Spanish by Merryn Williams)

I want to sleep the sleep of apples,
to leave behind the noise of cemeteries.
I want to sleep as did that child who wanted
to cut his heart on the high seas.

I do not want to hear again that corpses keep their blood,
nor of the thirst the rotting mouth can't slake.
I do not want to know of the torments grass gives,
nor of the moon with a snake's mouth
that toils before daybreak.

I want to sleep for a short time,
a short time, a minute, a hundred years;
but all should know that I have not died,
that there is a stable of gold on my lips,
that I am the friend of the west wind,
that I am the vast shadow of my tears.

Cover me with a veil,
throw fistfuls of ants at me at dawn,
and wet my shoes with hard water,
that it may slide on pincers like a scorpion.

Because I want to sleep the sleep of apples,
to learn a lament that will purify me;
because I want to stay with that dark child who wanted
to cut his heart on the high seas.

THEODORE ROETHKE
What Can I Tell My Bones?

1

Beginnner,
Perpetual beginner,
The soul knows not what to believe,
In its small folds, stirring sluggishly,
In the least place of its life,
A pulse beyond nothingness,
A fearful ignorance.

Before the moon draws back,
Dare I blaze like a tree?

In a world always late afternoon,
In the circular smells of a slow wind,
I listen to the weeds' vesperal whine,
Longing for absolutes that never come.
And shapes make me afraid:
The dance of natural objects in the mind,
The immediate sheen, the reality of straw,
The shadows crawling down a sunny wall.

A bird sings out in solitariness
A thin harsh song. The day dies in a child.
How close we are to the sad animals!
I need a pool; I need a puddle's calm.

O my bones,
Beware those perpetual beginnings,
Thinning the soul's substance;
The swan's dread of the darkening shore,
Or these insects pulsing near my skin,
The songs from a spiral tree.

Fury of wind, and no apparent wind,
A gust blowing the leaves suddenly upward,
A vine lashing in dry fury,
A man chasing a cat,
With a broken umbrella,
Crying softly.

2

It is difficult to say all things are well,
When the worst is about to arrive;
It is fatal to woo yourself,
However graceful the posture.

    Loved heart, what can I say?
    When I was a lark, I sang;
    When I was a worm, I devoured.

    The self says, I am;
    The heart says, I am less;
    The spirit says, you are nothing.

Mist alters the rocks. What can I tell my bones?
My desire's a wind trapped in a cave.
The spirit declares itself to these rocks.
I'm a small stone, loose in the shale.
Love is my wound.

The wide streams go their way,
The pond lapses back into a glassy silence.
The cause of God in me – has it gone?
Do these bones live? Can I live with these bones?
Mother, mother of us all, tell me where I am!
O to be delivered from the rational into the realm of pure song,
My face on fire, close to the points of a star,
A learned nimble girl,
Not drearily bewitched,
But sweetly daft.

    To try to become like God
    Is far from becoming God.
    O, but I seek and care!

    I rock in my own dark,
    Thinking, God has need of me.
    The dead love the unborn.

3

Weeds turn toward the wind weed-skeletons.
How slowly all things alter.
Existence dares perpetuate a soul,
A wedge of heaven's light, autumnal song.
I hear a beat of birds, the plangent wings
That disappear into a waning moon;
The barest speech of light among the stones.

To what more vast permission have I come?
When I walk past a vat, water joggles,
I no longer cry for green in the midst of cinders,
Or dream of the dead, and their holes.
Mercy has many arms.

Instead of a devil with horns, I prefer a serpent with scales;
In temptation, I rarely seek counsel;
A prisoner of smells, I would rather eat than pray.
I'm released from the dreary dance of opposites.
The wind rocks with my wish; the rain shields me;
I live in light's extreme; I stretch in all directions;
Sometimes I think I'm several.

The sun! The sun! And all we can become!
And the time ripe for running to the moon!
In the long fields, I leave my father's eye;
And shake the secrets from my deepest bones;
My spirit rises with the rising wind;
I'm thick with leaves and tender as a dove,
I take the liberties a short life permits –
I seek my own meekness;
I recover my tenderness by long looking.
By midnight I love everything alive.
Who took the darkness from the air?
I'm wet with another life.
Yea, I have gone and stayed.

What came to me vaguely is now clear,
As if released by a spirit,
Or agency outside me.
Unprayed-for,
And final.

ANNA AKHMATOVA
Dedication to *Requiem*
(translated from the Russian by Richard McKane)

The mountains bend before this grief,
the great river does not flow,
but the prison locks are strong,
and behind them the convict-holes,
and the anguish of death.
Someone basks in the sunset,
for someone the fresh wind blows.
We don't know, we are the same everywhere.
We only hear the repellent clank of keys,
the heavy steps of the soldiers.
We rose as though to early mass,
and went through the savage capital.
We used to meet each other there, more lifeless than the dead,
the sun lower, the Neva mistier,
but hope still sings in the distance.
Condemned...The sudden rush of tears.
One woman, already isolated from everyone else,
as though her life had been wrenched from her heart,
as though she had been smashed flat on her back,
she walks on...staggers...alone...
Where now are the captive companions
of my two hellish years?
What do they see in the Siberian blizzard,
what comes to them in the moon's circle?
I send them my farewell greeting.

ROBERT GRAVES
To Bring the Dead to Life

To bring the dead to life
Is no great magic.
Few are wholly dead:
Blow on a dead man's embers
And a live flame will start.

Let his forgotten griefs be now,
And now his withered hopes;
Subject your pen to his handwriting
Until it prove as natural
To sign his name as yours.

Limp as he limped,
Swear by the oaths he swore;
If he wore black, affect the same;
If he had gouty fingers,
Be yours gouty too.

Assemble tokens intimate of him –
A ring, a purse, a chair:
Around these elements then built
A home familiar to
The greedy revenant.

So grant him life, but reckon
That the grave which housed him
May not be empty now:
You in his spotted garments
Must yourself lie wrapped.

EDMOND JABÈS
Last Poem (untitled)
(translated from the French by Anthony Rudolf)

Look for my name in anthologies.
You will find it and you will not find it.
Look for my name in dictionaries.
You will find it and you will not find it.
Look for my name in encyclopaedias.
You will find it and you will not find it.
What does it matter? Have I ever had a name?
Therefore, when I die, do not
Look for my name in cemeteries
Or anywhere.
And stop tormenting now the one
Who cannot respond to the call.

ACKNOWLEDGEMENTS

Acknowledgements are due to the following publishers for their kind permission to reprint poems by these authors from their books: **Academy Chicago,** for Elinor Wylie; **Angus & Robertson Publishers,** for James McAuley from *Collected Poems* (1971); **Anvil Press Poetry Ltd,** for Carol Ann Duffy's 'Practising Being Dead' from *Selling Manhattan* (1987) and 'Dream of a Lost Friend' and 'Funeral' from *The Other Country* (1990), and 'Letter to My Mother' by Salvatore Quasimodo from *Complete Poems*, translated by Jack Bevan; **Black Sparrow Press,** for 'the twins', copyright © 1974 Charles Bukowski, from *Burning in Water Drowning in Flame: Selected Poems 1955-1973*; **Blackstaff Press,** for 'Cot' by Paul Durcan from *Daddy, Daddy* (1990), © Paul Durcan 1990; **BOA Editions Ltd,** 92 Park Avenue, Brockport, NY 14420, USA, for 'the lost baby poem' copyright © 1987 Lucille Clifton, from *Good Woman: Poems and a Memoir 1969-1980*; **Carcanet Press Ltd,** for Patricia Beer from *Selected Poems*, Elaine Feinstein from *Selected Poems*, Michael Haslam from *A Whole Bauble*, Mimi Khalvati from *Mirrorwork*, Hugh MacDiarmid from *Selected Poetry*, Ian McMillan from *Selected Poems*, Edna St Vincent Millay from *Selected Poems*, Les Murray from *Collected Poems*, John Crowe Ransom from *Selected Poems*, Peter Sansom from *Everything You've Heard Is True*, Mark Strand from *Selected Poems*, William Carlos Williams from *Collected Poems,* and David Wright from *Selected Poems*; **Ad. Donker,** Johannesburg, for Mandlenkosi Langa; **Enitharmon Press,** for Edwin Brock from *Five Ways to Kill a Man: New & Selected Poems* (1990), Jane Duran from *Breathe Now, Breathe* (1995), and David Gascoyne from *Selected Poems* (1995); **Faber & Faber Ltd,** for W.H. Auden from *Collected Poems* (1976), George Barker from *Collected Poems* (1987), John Berryman from *The Dream Songs* (1990), Alan Dugan from *Collected Poems* (1970), Douglas Dunn from *Elegies* (1985), Lawrence Durrell from *Collected Poems 1931-1974* (1980), W.S. Graham from *Collected Poems 1942-1977* (1979), Thom Gunn from *The Man with the Night Sweats* (1992), Seamus Heaney from *The Haw Lantern* (1987), Ted Hughes from *New Selected Poems 1957-1994* (1995), Andrew Motion from *Love in a Life* (1991), Paul Muldoon from *The Annals of Chile* (1994) and for his translation of 'The Mirror' by Michael Davitt from *Quoof* (1983), Theodore Roethke from *Collected Poems* (1968), and Derek Walcott from *Collected Poems* (1986); **The Gallery Press,** for Michael Coady from *Oven Lane* (1987), 'Anniversary' by Seán Dunne, Peter Fallon from *Eye to Eye* (1992), Michael Hartnett from *Selected and New Poems* (1992), Paula Meehan from *The Man who was Marked by Winter* (1991), and Frank Ormsby from *A Store of Candles* (1986); **Graywolf Press,** for John Haines; **HarperCollins Publishers,** New York, for Sterling A. Brown and Countee Cullen; **Harvard University Press,** for Emily Dickinson from *The Complete Poems of Emily Dickinson,* edited by Thomas H. Johnson; **The Harvill Press,** for 'Glocca Morra' by Paul Durcan from *A Snail in My Prime: New & Selected Poems* (Harvill Press, 1993), © Paul Durcan 1990, 1993; **Hippopotamus Press,** for 'A Dramatist Who Was My Father', 'Hospital Visit' and 'Visit' by Lotte Kramer from *A Lifelong House* (1983) and *The Shoemaker's Wife* (1987); **Henry Holt and Company, Inc,** for Erica Jong from *Half-Lives* (Holt, Rinehart and Winston, 1973); **John Hopkins University Press,** for Carol Bode; **Lagan Press,** for Robert Greacen; **Addison Wesley Longman Australia,** for Bruce Dawe from *Sometimes*

Gladness (1988); **Louisiana State University Press**, for John Stone; **The Mandeville Press**, for Katharine Middleton from *Water Lane*; **John Murray (Publishers) Ltd**, for John Betjeman from *Collected Poems*; **New Beacon Books**, for James Berry from *Fractured Circles* (1979); **Oxford University Press Ltd**, for Libby Houston from *A Stained Glass Raree Show* (Allison & Busby, 1967), Derek Mahon from *Poems 1962-1978* (1979), Peter Porter from *Collected Poems* (1983), Anne Stevenson from *Selected Poems 1956-1986* (1987); **Peepal Tree Press**, for John Figueroa and Marina Ama Omowale Maxwell; **Pelican Publishing Company**, for Aileen Campbell; **Penguin Books**, for Andrew Salkey; **Peterloo Poets**, for U.A. Fanthorpe, from *Standing To* (1982), Diana Hendry from *Call Making Blue* (1995), Michael Laskey from *Thinking of Happiness* (1991), and Ian McDonald from *Mercy Ward* (1988); **Random House UK Ltd**, for Milner Place from *In a Rare Time of Rain* (Chatto & Windus); **Reed Books**, for J.C. Hall from *Selected and New Poems 1939-1984* (Secker & Warburg, 1985) and Sharon Olds from *The Father* (Secker & Warburg, 1993); **Rockingham Press**, for Feyyaz Fergar from *A Talent for Shrouds*, Lotte Kramer from *Earthquake and other poems*, Oktay Rifat from *Voices of Memory: Selected Poems of Oktay Rifat*, translated by Ruth Christie, and Frances Wilson from *Close to Home*; **Seren Books**, for Christine Evans from *Cometary Phases* (1989); **Smith/Doorstop Books**, for Anna Fissler from *I Have No Mask* and Eleanor Maxted from *Paper Tiger*; **Souvenir Press Ltd**, for two translations by Alastair Reid from *Isla Negra* by Pablo Neruda; **Thelphini Press**, for Eleni Fourtouni from *Watch the Flame*; **International Thomson Publishing Services Ltd**, for Sidney Keyes from *Collected Poems* (Routledge, 1988); **Virago Press**, for Grace Nichols from *The Fat Black Woman's Poems* and Anne Sexton from *Complete Poems*; **University of Virginia Press**, for Paul Laurence Dunbar from *Collected Poems*.

Acknowledgements are due to the following authors and translators or their executors for poems from books published by **Bloodaxe Books Ltd**: Elizabeth Bartlett from *Two Women Dancing: New & Selected Poems* (1995), Martin Bell from *Complete Poems* (1988), Ron Butlin from *Histories of Desire* (1995), Brendan Cleary from *The Irish Card* (1993), David Constantine from *Selected Poems* (1991), Maura Dooley from *Kissing a Bone* (1996), Lauris Edmond from *New & Selected Poems* (1992), Roy Fisher from *The Dow Low Drop: New & Selected Poems* (1996), Tony Flynn from *A Strange Routine* (1980), Linda France from *Red* (1992) and *The Gentleness of the Very Tall* (1994), Tess Gallagher from *My Black Horse: New & Selected Poems* (1995), Pamela Gillilan from *All-Steel Traveller: New & Selected Poems* (1994), Frances Horovitz from *Collected Poems* (1985), Brendan Kennelly from *A Time for Voices: Selected Poems 1960-1990* (1990), Marion Lomax from *Raiding the Borders* (1996), Richard McKane for 'Dedication to *Requiem*' from *Anna Akhmatova: Selected Poems* (1989), Ruth Padel from *Angel* (1993), Ann Sansom from *Romance* (1994), Matt Simpson, from *An Elegy for the Galosherman: New & Selected Poems* (1990), Ken Smith from *Tender to the Queen of Spain* (1993), R.S. Thomas, from *Selected Poems 1946-1968* (1986), John Hartley Williams from *Double* (1994), C.K. Williams from *New & Selected Poems* (1995), and Merryn Williams for three translations from *Federico García Lorca: Selected Poems* (1992);

Acknowledgements are due to the following literary agents, estates and executors for their kind permission to reprint work by these authors: **Curtis Brown Ltd**, for X.J. Kennedy from *Nude Descending a Staircase* (1961), copyright © 1960 by X.J. Kennedy, renewed, first appeared in *The New Yorker*; **Gordon Dickerson**, for Tony Harrison from *Selected Poems* (Penguin Books, 1987); **Agneta Falk**, for Asa Benveniste from *Invisible Ink* (Singing Horse Press/Branch Redd Books, 1989); **David Godwin Associates**, for Ben Okri from *An African Elegy* (Jonathan Cape, 1992); **David Higham Associates Ltd**, for Paul Hyland from *The Stubborn Forest* (Bloodaxe Books, 1984), Elizabeth Jennings from *Collected Poems* (Carcanet, 1986) and *Times and Seasons* (Carcanet, 1992), Michael Longley from *Poems 1963-1983* (Secker & Warburg, 1991), Alasdair Maclean from *Waking the Dead* (Gollancz, 1976), Louis MacNeice from *Collected Poems* (Faber, 1966), and Dylan Thomas, from *The Poems*; **Sheil Land Associates**, for Dannie Abse and George MacBeth; **Peake Associates**, for Alison Fell; **Rogers, Coleridge & White Ltd** for Adrian Henri, from *Wish You Were Here* (Jonathan Cape, 1990), copyright © Adrian Henri 1990, and Edward Lucie-Smith, from *A Tropical Childhood and other poems* (Oxford University Press, 1961), copyright © Edward Lucie-Smith 1961; **William L. Rukeyser**, for 'Eighth Elegy. Children's Elegy' by Muriel Rukeyser, from *A Muriel Rukeyser Reader* (W.W. Norton, New York, 1994), © William L. Rukeyser; **Richard Scott Simon Ltd**, for James Wright from *Above the River: Complete Poems* (Bloodaxe Books, 1992); **Abner Stein**, for Marvin Bell, James Dickey and Robert Pack; **A.P. Watt Ltd**, for Robert Graves; **Sarah White**, for Eric W. White.

Acknowledgements are due to the following authors and translators to reprint poems from these books: **Peter Abbs**, from *Icons of Time* (Gryphon Press); **Robert Bly**, for his translation (with John Knoepfle) from *Twenty Poems of César Vallejo* (The Sixties Press, 1962); **Fred D'Aguiar**, from *Airy Hall* (Chatto & Windus, 1989); **John F. Deane**, from *The Stylised City: New & Selected Poems* (Dedalus Press, 1991); **D.J. Enright**, from *Collected Poems 1987* (Oxford University Press, 1987); **David H.W. Grubb**, from *Turtle Mythologies* (University of Salzburg Press); **Jack Hirschman**, from *Endless Threshold*; **Philip Hodgins**, from *Blood and Bone* (Angus & Robertson, 1986); **Rupert M. Loydell**, from *Timber Across the Sun* (University of Salzburg Press); **Dennis O'Driscoll**, from *Hidden Extras* (Anvil Press Poetry, 1987); **Olive Senior**, from *Talking of Trees* (Calabash, Jamaica, 1985); **John Smith**, from *Entering Rooms* (Chatto & Windus, 1973).

Thanks are due to **Anthony Rudolf** for the following: his own poem 'Old Man', first published as a poemcard by Los, © Anthony Rudolf 1981; 'A Phonecall from New York', translation © Anthony Rudolf 1992, first published in *Flow Tide: Selected Poetry and Prose* by Claude Vigée, edited and translated by Anthony Rudolf (Menard/King's College London, 1992); 'Last Poem' by Edmond Jabès, translation © Anthony Rudolf 1991, first published in *Temenos* and *The Jewish Quarterly*; 'Eyes' by Evgeny Vinokourov, translation © Anthony Rudolf 1976, first published in *After the War: Selected Poems of Evgeny Vinokourov*, edited and translated by Anthony Rudolf (Carcanet Press, 1976).

Permission to reprint all other poems has been obtained or sought from the authors concerned, who reserve all copyright on those poems. Every effort has been made to trace copyright holders of material included in this book. The editors and publisher apologise if any material has been included without permission or without the appropriate acknowledgement, and would be glad to be told of anyone who has not been consulted.

INDEX OF TITLES & FIRST LINES

(titles are in italics, first lines in roman type)

INDEX OF POETS & TRANSLATORS